Lecture Notes in Computer Science

T0238361

Commenced Publication in 1973
Founding and Former Series Editors:
Gerhard Goos, Juris Hartmanis, and Jan van Leeuwen

Editorial Board

Yun Q. Shi (Ed.)

Transactions on Data Hiding and Multimedia Security IV

 Springer

Volume Editor

Yun Q. Shi
New Jersey Institute of Technology
University Heights, Newark, NJ 07102-1982, USA
E-mail: shi@njit.edu

Library of Congress Control Number: Applied for

CR Subject Classification (1998): K.4.1, K.6.5, H.5.1, D.4.6, E.3, E.4, F.2.2, H.3, I.4

ISSN 0302-9743 (Lecture Notes in Computer Science)
ISSN 1864-3043 (Transactions on Data Hiding and Multimedia Security)

ISBN 978-3-642-01756-8 Springer Berlin Heidelberg New York

springer.com

© Springer-Verlag Berlin Heidelberg 2009

Typesetting: Camera-ready by author, data conversion by Scientific Publishing Services, Chennai, India
Printed on acid-free paper   SPIN: 12678990   06/3180   5 4 3 2 1 0

Preface

In this volume we present the fourth issue of the *LNCS Transactions on Data Hiding and Multimedia Security* containing five papers on digital watermarking.

The first three papers deal with robust watermarking. In the first paper, Piper and Safavi-Naini address the issue of how many images should be used in experiments to evaluate the robustness of watermarking algorithms in order to have confidence in the experimental results. A statistical approach based on hypothesis testing and power analysis is provided to determine this number. The second paper, by X. Qi and J. Qi, proposes a content-based desynchronization resilient watermarking scheme, which combines the advantages of feature extraction, perceptual analysis, one-way hash functions, and spread-spectrum-based blind watermark embedding and retrieval. In the third paper, Liu and Tsai present a new robust watermark for presentation slides that employs blank space coloring. The embedded watermark is resilient against many common modifications applied to slides. The fourth paper, by Jiang et al., presents a new least distortion linear gain model for halftone image watermarking that incorporates perceptual quality metrics. In the last paper, Xuan et al. presents an optimal histogram pair-based image-reversible data-hiding scheme.

We hope that this issue is of great interest to the research community and will trigger new research in the field of data hiding and multimedia security.

Finally, we want to thank all the authors, reviewers, and editors who have devoted their valuable time to the success of this fourth issue. Special thanks goes to Springer and Alfred Hofmann for their continuous support.

March 2009

Yun Q. Shi
(Editor-in-Chief)
Hyoung-Joong Kim
(Vice Editor-in-Chief)
Stefan Katzenbeisser
(Vice Editor-in-Chief)

Table of Contents

How to Compare Image Watermarking Algorithms

Angela Piper[1] and Reihaneh Safavi-Naini[2,*]

[1] School of IT and CS
University of Wollongong
Australia
[2] Dept. of Computer Science
University of Calgary
Canada

Abstract. In recent years, comparing image watermarking algorithms using the results of experiments with a handful of images has become a common practice. The images are randomly selected from a well chosen database and so it can be argued that they cover the important aspects of visual information such as texture or smoothness. However, the number of images used in the experiment remains a crucial factor in providing confidence in the results of experiment. By choosing this number to be 'large' one *hopes* that the comparison results are reliable. In this paper, our aim is to provide a systematic method of determining this number using a statistical approach based on hypothesis testing and power analysis.

We consider two algorithms and seek to verify the claim that one has superior performance with respect to some property. We start with finding a measure that represents the 'goodness' of the property of interest, follow with determining a suitable hypothesis test and the number of images and, finally, with interpreting the results of the experiment. We show how the use of a statistical framework can allow us not only to draw conclusions based on a sound methodology but also to provide a confidence level for these conclusions. We give a concrete application of the approach to the problem of comparing two spread spectrum watermarking algorithms with respect to their robustness to JPEG2000 compression. We discuss the intricacies of the choices at various stages of this approach, and their effects on the results.

1 Introduction

Digital Watermarking embeds a digital signal, known as a watermark, into an image (or other digital content) with the aim of being able to detect it at a later

---

* The majority of this work was completed while Reihaneh Safavi-Naini was at the School of IT and CS, Univeristy of Wollongong, Australia. Partial funding for this research was provided by the Smart Internet Technology Cooperative Research Centre, Australia.

Y.Q. Shi (Ed.): Transactions on DHMS IV, LNCS 5510, pp. 1–28, 2009.

stage. In the intervening period, the watermarked image can undergo various forms of processing. A watermarking system is robust if it can successfully detect the watermark in the processed image.

Watermark robustness is an important requirement in many applications and so an important step in the evaluation of a new watermarking system is to demonstrate its robustness and in particular in comparison to other systems.

Although some work has been done towards theoretical comparisons, the dominant approach for comparing watermarking algorithms is through well designed experiments. In this case each watermarking algorithm is applied to the same set of images. The watermarked images are then subjected to processing (or attack); an algorithm is considered more robust than another if its watermarks are more detectable in the processed images.

Since the set of images used for the comparison is only a subset of all possible images to which the watermarking algorithms could be applied, the comparison outcome may not reliably reflect the difference in the algorithms' robustness but be a chance result due to the chosen image set.

This means that the number and types of images used in the set needs to be carefully determined. If a small number of images is used, there is a higher probability that the outcome does not reflect the real robustness difference and will be influenced by the properties of the test images. On the other hand, it is desirable to use the smallest possible set to minimize the required computation.

It is not immediately clear what the 'right' number of images is. The existing choices in the literature appear to be ad hoc. Some papers use as few as two or three test images [1, 2] and others use hundreds [3, 4] without any justification in either case. Even benchmarking papers that focus on the problems of robustness comparison, do not discuss the choice of the number of images and its effect on the reliability of the results.

Benchmarking systems are often accompanied by a worked example or an image database, so we could use that number of images as a guide, but this number also varies: [5] obtain their results from 4 images, [6] uses 16 audio files, [7] provide 29 images and, at the other extreme, the system in [8] has a public version with 1301 images, and an internal research version comprising at least 5000.

One cannot expect to determine a 'right' number of images that would be appropriate for all comparisons, as robustness differences between algorithms will be more or less difficult to discern depending on the attacks, robustness measure and algorithms themselves. However, we do require a more systematic approach than following either the choice made in an existing paper or our own intuition.

1.1   A Statistical Framework for Robustness Comparison

In this paper we develop a statistical approach to determining the required number of images for robustness comparison of watermarking algorithms. Although we describe our approach in relation to robustness comparison, it can be appropriately modified for comparing other properties of watermarking algorithms.

We first give a quantitative definition of robustness and examine how it can be measured. To fully compare the robustness of watermarking systems would require a measurement from every (image, key) pair. The aim of the statistical approach is to measure robustness on only a subset of images and keys, called the 'sample set', and be able to draw conclusions, while maintaining some level of confidence in these conclusions.

Hypothesis testing is a formal method for drawing conclusions by deciding between two competing claims (or hypotheses) based on measurements on a sample taken from the whole population, in this case measurements of algorithm robustness taken from he set of test images. By selecting an appropriate hypothesis test and applying it to the sample set, we can estimate which algorithm is more robust and also the probability of the observed difference between algorithms occurring by chance. If this probability is low, we can conclude that one algorithm is more robust than the other.

Requiring the probability to be low limits the chance of erroneously concluding that a difference in robustness exists. However this may cause us to erroneously conclude that no difference in robustness exists. Increasing the size of the sample set can overcome this problem, allowing both types of errors to be reduced; however the use of too large a sample can waste considerable amounts of time and resources. *Power analysis* is a method for determining the size of the sample set required for a hypothesis test in which both types of error are limited to specified levels.

Once the 'right' number of images is determined, a measurement process can be applied to the test image set to produce a set of measurements. These measurements form the sample set for the hypothesis test. It is important to use an appropriate test. The test that was originally planned may have to be replaced with a different one. This may occur, for example, when the assumptions required by the test are not satisfied by the sample data.

Finally, the results of statistical tests need to be interpreted; a positive test result does not necessarily mean that one algorithm will greatly improve robustness or improve robustness in all possible applications. Raw results may be made more meaningful by relating them back to the original problem of watermark detection.

1.2   Case Study

We implement the approach outlined above for comparing two zero-bit, spread spectrum watermarking algorithms in terms of their robustness to JPEG2000 compression. In addition to hypothesis testing and power analysis, we examine all phases of the comparison and highlight some of the complexities involved, such as choosing a good robustness measurement, ensuring that the embedding process is fair and identifying, and recovering from, failed test assumptions.

Although the decisions we make are centred on our particular case study, most watermarking comparisons will confront similar issues and be faced with similar choices. The particular algorithms used in our case study are non-blind and the particular claim that interests us is robustness to JPEG2000, however blind algorithms can be evaluated without altering the method, as can robustness to other attacks, or indeed any claim for which an appropriate performance measure (see Sect. 3) can be devised.[1]

Both of the watermarking algorithms in our case study operate in the discrete wavelet domain and use the same coefficient selection criteria to determine the set of coefficients where the watermark will be embedded. However the first algorithm NoHVS uses a fixed watermark strength ω, while the second algorithm HVS uses an adaptive watermark strength ω_i adjusted according to the frequency and texture sensitivities of the human visual system (see appendix B for algorithm details).

JPEG2000 [9] (outlined in Sect. 2.2) is a scalable compression scheme that allows different types of compression; the two most important being *resolution* and *quality* compression. The claim we wish to investigate is that the HVS algorithm will have superior robustness to quality compression while maintaining robustness to resolution compression. Thus we use two comparisons between our algorithms, one which examines quality compression and the other which examines resolution compression. Experimental results show that the HVS algorithm provides a substantial increase in robustness to quality compression with a slight, but not substantial, reduction in robustness to resolution compression.

The paper is organised as follows. Section 2 provides background information on watermarking and JPEG2000 compression. Section 3 discusses some concepts in robustness measurement and section 4 describes hypothesis testing and power analysis. Assumption verification and interpretation of results are discussed in section 5. Section 6 outlines the main steps in the comparison framework and details the decisions made for our case study at each of these steps. This includes the power analysis, hypothesis test, results and conclusions on the comparative robustness of HVS and NoHVS. Some final remarks on watermark comparison using this framework can be found in section 7.

1.3 Related Work

While the framework presented in this paper is for the experimental comparison of watermarking algorithms, some work has been done towards theoretical algorithm comparison.

Su et al. [10] compare the robustness of watermarking algorithms to white noise addition and to optimum linear filtering. They use theoretical models for both the image (or other signal) and watermark. However, it is not clear how applicable such results would be for real images nor that it is necessarily possible to apply this approach for more complex types of processing. Adelsbach et al. [11] work towards formal definitions of watermark robustness. They suggest that further work may, eventually, lead to reductionist proofs based on hard problems as can be found in cryptography. Such proofs would provide a basis for algorithm

---

[1] While our method can be used for different types of algorithms, such as zero-bit and multi-bit or blind and non-blind, comparison across algorithm types is rarely desirable. Not only can it be difficult to identify a performance measure which is appropriate for both types of algorithm but also an intended application is typically best suited by only a single type of algorithm.

comparison, however it is clear that more development is needed before this theoretical approach will be viable.

More closely associated with the framework presented here are the many experimental comparisons of watermarking algorithms. Although our experimental approach is similar in many regards to these works, we use statistical methods to determine an appropriate number of images for reliable results, whereas there are, to our knowledge, no such papers discussing the effects of the size of the image set on result reliability.

Early work on Stirmark by Kutter and Petitcolas [7] describes an experimental structure, applying a set of attacks to each of a set of images watermarked with a fixed payload at a fixed visual quality and measuring the detection outcome, that is used essentially unchanged today. Fridrich and Goljan [5] present a similar method for watermark comparison, but allow minor modifications to watermarking algorithms so that they may be compared using both a zero-bit and a 60-bit payload. Yet, although both papers note that the properties of the test images will influence the outcome and thus a varied test set should be used, neither mentions the effect of the number of images upon the reliability of the test results.

Further advances including Checkmark by Pereira et al. [12] and Optimark by Solachidis et al. [13], both of which suggest additional attacks and weighting of results towards specific applications, largely ignore this issue. While [13] does state that the number of keys has an effect on the accuracy of results, nothing is mentioned about the required number of images. Macq, Dittmann and Delp [14], focus on the need for modularity and accessability in benchmarking tools and for effective objective image quality measures but do not discuss the effect of the size of the test set on confidence in the results.

Papers from Kim et al. [8] and Kim and Delp [15], on the Watermark Evaluation Testbed suggest that future work should involve the extension of the results to include confidence levels. This shows that the authors are aware that reliability of results should be a factor in experimental comparison, even though neither paper provides a method for including this.

Recent work by Dittman et al. [6] considers the comparison of audio watermarking algorithms. They eschew payload and watermarking induced distortion standardisation in order to plot the tradeoff between payload, robustness and imperceptability obtained by each particular algorithm and choice of parameters. Once again, no mention is made of the effects of the test set size on result reliability.

2 Preliminaries

2.1 Watermarking

A digital watermarking system X consists of an *embedding* and a *detection* algorithm.

The *embedding* algorithm takes an image (or other media item) I, a message M, and a secret key k and produces a watermarked image I' by imperceptibly altering the content of I.

$$I'_{X,M,k} = Embed_X(I, M, k).$$

Embedding algorithms typically use an *embedding strength* parameter. Increasing the embedding strength will increase detectability of the watermark at the cost of greater distortion.

The *detection* algorithm takes a candidate image I^c, the key k and, optionally, the original image I and outputs *True* and the message, or *False* if no watermark has been detected.

$$Detect(I^c, I, k) = \begin{cases} \{True, M\} & \text{if } I^c \text{ was watermarked with key } k \\ \{False\} & \text{otherwise.} \end{cases}$$

A watermarking system may produce incorrect results. Some images may appear to contain a watermark when none has been embedded, and in some images it may not be possible to embed a watermark which is both detectable and imperceptible. Finally, processing of an image may cause the detection algorithm to fail.

The detection algorithm $Detect_X(I^c, I, k)$ results in one of four outcomes, depending on whether or not the watermark was embedded and detected in the candidate image I^c (table 1).

Table 1. Classification of watermarking outcomes

		Watermark Embedded	
		Yes	**No**
Watermark	**Yes**	True Positive	False Positive
Detected	**No**	False Negative	True Negative

Let $I'_{X,M,k} = Embed_X(I, M, k)$ and $I^F_{X,M,k}$ denote a modified version of $I'_{X,M,k}$ obtained through the application of some (possibly null) process F. We say that the watermark is *detectable in the image* $I^F_{X,M,k}$ if applying the detection algorithm correctly produces the output

$$Detect_X(I^F_{X,M,k}, I, k) = \{True, M\}.$$

The *detectability* of a watermarking system X under processing F is the probability, taken over all original images I, messages M and keys k, that the watermark is detectable in the image $I^F_{X,M,k}$.

$$P(Detect_X(I^F_{X,M,k}, I, k) = \{True, M\}).$$

The *robustness* of a watermarking system X under processing F is the probability, taken over all original images I, messages M and keys k, that F does not affect the detectability of the watermark.

$$P(Detect_X(I^F_{X,k}, I, k) = Detect_X(I'_{X,k}, I, k))$$

A watermark is *imperceptible* if the distortion caused by the embedding algorithm is not noticeable to a human observer.

Imperceptibility is achieved through the use of a *perceptual model*, which is an abstraction of the human visual system[2] and is used to describe the perceptibility of the changes to the original image due to watermark embedding.

In some systems formal perceptual models are used [16,17], while others rely on implicit models. For example the embedding systems in [18] and [19] assume that 'any pixel modification not exceeding some constant c is imperceptible'.

A *perceptual distortion measure*[3] D_W quantifies the amount of distortion in accordance with some perceptual model. Let l_W be a distortion threshold. A watermark is *imperceptible* in an image $I'_{X,M,k} = Embed(I, M, k)$ if

$$D_W(I, I'_{X,M,k}) < l_W.$$

The *payload* of a watermarking system is the message size, measured in bits, embedded using the watermark.

Many watermarking algorithms are developed to embed zero-bit watermarks. In *zero-bit* watermarking systems no message is embedded and the detection algorithm only detects the existence of the watermark. Embedding a larger payload will reduce the robustness if the same level of imperceptibility is maintained.

A Spread Spectrum Watermarking Algorithm. The two algorithms considered in this paper are both zero-bit spread spectrum watermarking algorithms. The following outlines the embedding and detection components of a basic zero-bit spread spectrum watermarking algorithm such as the one described by Cox et al. [20].

Embedding

Input: I, k, N, ω
Output: I'
○ Use the secret key k to generate a pseudorandom sequence $W = (w_1, w_2, ..., w_N)$, where $w_i \in \mathbb{R}$ is normally distributed with mean 0 and variance 1
○ Transform I using a frequency transform such as the discrete cosine transform
○ Set $I' = I$
○ Select the N coefficients $V = (v_1, v_2, ..., v_N)$ from I which have the highest absolute magnitudes
○ Select corresponding coefficients $V' = (v'_1, v'_2, ..., v'_N)$ from I'
○ Modify I' so that $v'_i = v_i + \omega w_i \quad 1 \le i \le N$

---

[2] Human visual system models are the relevant perceptual models for images. Which perceptual system is abstracted depends on how the watermarked signal is consumed. Watermarking music or speech will require auditory system models, while watermarked video may use both.

[3] See Sect. 3.3 for a discussion of the problems with perceptual distortion measurement.

Detection

Input: I^c, I, k, N, ω
Output: $\{True\}$ or $\{False\}$
∘ Use k to generate $W = (w_1, w_2, ..., w_N)$ as for **Embedding**
∘ Transform I and I^c as for **Embedding**
∘ Select $V = (v_1, v_2, ..., v_N)$ from I as for **Embedding**
∘ Select corresponding coefficients, i.e. those having the same indices in the transformed image, $(v_1^c, v_2^c, ..., v_N^c)$ from I^c
∘ Extract $W^c = (w_1^c, w_2^c, ..., w_N^c)$ where $w_i^c = \frac{1}{\omega}(\frac{v_i^c}{v_i} - 1)$
∘ Calculate $\gamma(I^c, I, k) = sim(W^c, W) = \frac{W^c \cdot W}{\sqrt{W^c \cdot W^c}}$
∘ Compare $\gamma(I^c, I, k)$ to a *detection threshold* T and output
$Detect(I^c, I, k) = \begin{cases} \{True\} & \text{if } \gamma(I^c, I, k) > T \\ \{False\} & \text{otherwise} \end{cases}$

2.2 JPEG2000

JPEG2000 [9] is a wavelet-based image compression standard. It allows an image to be compressed by quality and by resolution.

In *resolution compression* a discrete wavelet transform (DWT) is applied to the image using a dyadic decomposition structure. The lowest resolution layer is formed from the LL subband after N_L decompositions. Each subsequent resolution layer contains the LH, HL and HH subbands required to double the horizontal and vertical image resolutions. By retaining a number of the lowest resolution layers, a resolution compressed image can be produced.

In *quality compression*, the wavelet coefficients are coded in a number of *coding passes*. Each pass encodes a single bit each[4] from some of the coefficients. Passes are arranged into layers so that the greatest quality improvements are in the lowest layer, those with slightly smaller improvements appear in the next layer and so on. A quality compressed image is produced by retaining a number of the lowest quality layers.

3   Measuring Robustness

In the definition of robustness in Sect. 2.1, probability over all messages, images and keys is considered. We restrict ourselves to zero-bit watermarks and define a robustness measure for a single image I over a set of keys K. Averaging over keys will be necessary for correct application of our particular hypothesis test because, while it is possible to measure all pairs of image I and key k separately, sample points with the same I would violate the independence assumption (Sect. 6.1) required by our chosen test. The measure can then be applied to a set of images $\mathcal{I}$ to generate the sample data for the hypothesis test (Sect. 4). We consider two measures of robustness, the *true positive rate* and the *detection statistic*.

---

[4] If the bit encoded for a given coefficient is the most significant bit of that coefficient, an additional bit representing the sign of the coefficient will also be encoded.

The robustness of a watermarking system X to processing F for the image I can be estimated by generating $I'_{X,k}$ and $I^F_{X,k}$ for a set of secret keys K and and calculating the proportion of keys for which

$$Detect_X(I^F_{X,k}, I, k) = Detect_X(I'_{X,k}, I, k).$$

It is usually assumed that given the correct key, an algorithm will correctly detect a watermark from the unmodified watermarked image

$$Detect_X(I'_{X,k}, I, k) = \{True\}, \ \forall I'_{X,k} = Embed_X(I, k),$$

which should be valid in any good watermarking system. This equates robustness with detectability, allowing measurement using the true positive rate.

3.1 True Positive Rate

To measure the *true positive rate* of algorithm X after processing F for the image I over a set of keys K we generate

$$I^F_{X,k} = F(Embed_X(I, k)) \qquad \forall k \in K$$

and calculate

$$tp_X(I, F) = \frac{|\{k \in K : Detect(I^F_{X,k}, I, k) = \{True\}\}|}{|K|}.$$

However, in robust watermarking systems, the false negative probability may be extremely low, requiring a large number of detection attempts before there is enough accuracy for a reasonable comparison of true positive rates.

3.2 Detection Statistic

In true positive rate measurement each trial has a binary outcome, detectable or not detectable, due to thresholding γ (Sect. 2.1). The thresholding loses information that is useful for robustness measurement. The mean detection statistic is a robustness measure which retains this information, although it is an indirect measurement and thus harder to interpret.

For this we generate

$$I^F_{X,k} = F(Embed_X(I, k)) \qquad \forall k \in K$$

and calculate

$$ds_X(I, F) = \frac{\sum_{k \in K} \gamma(I^F_{X,k}, I, k)}{|K|}.$$

This measure is only suitable for comparing systems which use the same detection statistic and associated threshold. A higher mean detection statistic does not automatically imply a higher true positive rate, as it relies on the assumption that the the detection statistic has the same shaped distribution for each algorithm.

3.3   Fair Embedding

A trade-off exists between the perceptibility of a watermark and its robustness and for fair comparison watermarks must be embedded at the same level of perceptibility. Thus for every trial the embedding strength of each algorithm must be adjusted to result in equal perceptual distortion. There are two ways of measuring perceptual distortion: subjective measurement and objective measurement.

In subjective measurements the imperceptibility of a watermark (Sect. 2.1) is defined in terms of a human observer. Since human perception is not exactly the same for all observers, in practice a group of observers is used to obtain a result which reflects perceptibility of the 'average' observer.

While subjective measurement is arguably the best method of equalising the watermark-induced distortion, the process is time consuming; in practice only a limited number of images can be used. A computed perceptibility measure is not only faster but allows reproducibility for any researchers wishing to verify the results. Unfortunately, there is no standard measurement which is agreed upon by the watermarking community.

The peak signal to noise ratio (PSNR) is a simple and commonly used measurement but the inadequacy of this measure, like all mean squared error based measures, for perceptibility has been well documented [21, 22]. More sophisticated measures, such as the S-CIELAB metric [23], use models of the human visual system and are thus better correlated with the perceptibility evaluations of human observers. Such measures require the viewing conditions to be specified and so the perceptibility metric and any relevant viewing condition information should be stated in addition to the target level of distortion for the embedding procedure.

We note that the choice of objective measure can bias the results. The more closely aligned the chosen perceptual distortion measure is with the perceptual model of a watermarking system, the better that system is likely to perform. In the extreme case, when the watermarking algorithm and the distortion measure use the same model, the watermarking algorithm will embed most strongly in precisely the manner judged least perceptible by the measure and so will perform better compared to a second algorithm that uses a different perceptual model.

This problem cannot be easily resolved as it is natural that the models used in watermarking will align with those used in image quality evaluation. The best that can be done is to ensure that the perceptual distortion measures used for evaluation are well correlated with subjective measures of perceptibility.

4   Statistical Methods for Robustness Comparison

To measure the robustness of a given watermarking system A a set of test images $\mathcal{I}$ is used. For each image in $\mathcal{I}$ a robustness measurement is performed, resulting in a set of measurements $\mathcal{A}$. Applying the same process for algorithm B will yield a set $\mathcal{B}$ (see section 6, steps 3–6).

The aim is to compare the relative robustness of A and B for the population of images $\mathcal{I}_u$, that is the set of images of interest, using the measurements from the application of the two algorithms on the test images $\mathcal{I} \subset \mathcal{I}_u$. Let $\mathcal{A}_u$ and $\mathcal{B}_u$ denote the robustness measurements for algorithms A and B on the entire population $\mathcal{I}_u$, then $\mu_a = \sum_{a \in \mathcal{A}_u} \frac{a}{|\mathcal{A}_u|}$ and $\mu_b = \sum_{b \in \mathcal{B}_u} \frac{b}{|\mathcal{B}_u|}$ denote the *population means* for algorithms A and B respectively.

We say that algorithm A is more robust than algorithm B in the population of interest if $\mu_a - \mu_b > 0$[5]. Direct comparison of μ_a and μ_b would require the (potentially infinite) sets $\mathcal{A}_u$ and $\mathcal{B}_u$ to be generated. Instead, we compare the *sample means* $m_a = \sum_{a \in \mathcal{A}} \frac{a}{|\mathcal{A}|}$ and $m_b = \sum_{b \in \mathcal{B}} \frac{b}{|\mathcal{B}|}$.

If $m_a - m_b > 0$, we can conclude that algorithm A is more robust than algorithm B (and vice versa). This method of comparison does not provide any assurance that the observed difference in means is not simply a chance result of the images used in the sample. *Hypothesis testing* is the method by which we obtain such an assurance.

4.1   Hypothesis Testing

Statistical hypothesis testing [24] is a method for deciding between two competing hypotheses: the null hypothesis H_0, which conventionally states that the observed result is entirely due to chance, and the alternative hypothesis H_1, which conventionally states that the result is due to a real difference between the populations $\mathcal{A}_u$ and $\mathcal{B}_u$.

Hypothesis testing requires the selection of a hypothesis test and evaluation of a *test statistic t*, calculated from the sample measurements. If the value of t obtained is sufficiently unlikely under H_0, we entertain the alternative hypotheis H_1.

Provided $\mathcal{A}_u$ and $\mathcal{B}_u$ satisfy a set of assumptions, t will have a known probability distribution when H_0 is true. (The assumptions and the associated distribution of the test statistic will depend on chosen hypothesis test.) This distribution is used to calculate a p-value, which is the probability p of obtaining a value of t that is less supportive of H_0 than the value obtained from the sample measurements. If this p-value is below some *significance level* α we reject H_0 in favour of H_1. If H_0 is rejected, we say that the observed difference is *significant*, which suggests it is not due to chance.

The *confidence* and *power* of a test are determined by two parameters, α and β. The choice of α defines the probability of erroneously rejecting H_0 and establishes the *confidence level* $1 - \alpha$, which is the probability of correctly accepting H_0. The probability of *erroneously accepting* H_0 is β. This probability also determines the *power* $1 - \beta$ of the test, which is the probability of correctly rejecting H_0. The probabilities α and β are also known as the type-I and type-II error rates.

---

[5] Comparing means is not always sufficient. For example, we may prefer a system which performs reasonably well on all images over an algorithm which performs extremely well on some images but not at all well on others. If the distributions of $\mathcal{A}_u$ and $\mathcal{B}_u$ have similar shape and spread we can expect their means μ_a and μ_b to provide a fair comparison of robustness.

If α is small, we can be confident that any significant difference is not simply due to the image set. However, *for a fixed number of images*, there is a trade-off between α and β. So small values of α will cause large values of β. To obtain low values for both α and β the number of images n must be increased. *Power analysis* is concerned with the relationship between the sample size n, and the error probabilities α and β. The formulae it provides can be used to determine how many images are required to maintain acceptably low error probabilities.

Applying hypothesis testing to the secnario described in Sect. 4 we derive null and alternative hypotheses.[6] The null hypothesis asserts that any observed differences are due *only to chance*. That is, that the mean robustness is the same for both algorithms:

$$H_0 : \mu_a = \mu_b.$$

The alternative hypothesis asserts that observed differences are due to *underlying differences in the population*. That is, the mean robustness of one algorithm is greater than the other:

$$H_1 : \mu_a \neq \mu_b.$$

The calculation of the test statistic and its associated p-values depends upon the chosen hypothesis test. The most widely known test for these hypotheses is the two sample t-test (see appendix A). In watermarking experiments, however, we can watermark identical copies of the image I_i with systems A and B. This suggests the use of the more powerful paired t-test, which takes advantage of the natural pairing between watermark robustness measurements a_i and b_i taken from the same image I_i.

The Paired t-test. To perform the paired t-test we find the sample mean m_d and standard error SE_d of the differences $d_i = a_i - b_i$ between our sample measurements. and calculate the test statistic

$$t_d = \frac{m_d}{SE_d}$$

which, if H_0 is true, will have student's-t distribution with $\nu = n - 1$ degrees of freedom. The further t_d is from zero, the less it supports the null hypothesis.

The p-value is the probability[7] that a test statistic t drawn from the student's-t distribution t_ν is further from zero than t_d

$$p = P(t \sim t_\nu > |t_d|) + P(t \sim t_\nu < -|t_d|)$$
$$= 2 \times P(t \sim t_\nu > t_d).$$

If $p < \alpha$, we reject H_0 with confidence $1 - \alpha$ and conclude that there is a significant difference in robustness between algorithms A and B. If $p \geq \alpha$ we conclude that neither algorithm is significantly better than the other.

---

[6] This will result in a two-sided hypothesis test as H_1 includes both the situation where $\mu_a > \mu_b$ and where $\mu_a < \mu_b$. We use this rather than a one-sided hypothesis test to allow for the possibility that our new algorithm has substantially worse robustness than the original.

[7] The notation $P(s \sim D > v)$ represents the probability that a sample s, drawn randomly from distribution D, has a value greater than v.

4.2   Power Analysis

Power analysis is used to determine the appropriate sample size for the hypothesis test. That is, the smallest number of images n which will keep both the type-I error rate α and the type-II error rate β low.

The size of the sample will be dependent on the allowable error rates, the standard deviation of the sample values and the size of the difference in means that we wish to detect.

For a paired t-test, if the difference in population means is δ and the standard deviation of the difference values is σ_d, then the number of images required to achieve error rates α and β is given by:

$$n \geq \frac{\sigma_d^2}{\delta^2}(t_{\alpha(2),n-1} + t_{\beta(1),n-1})^2 \tag{1}$$

where $t_{x(y),\nu}$ is the value such that the probability that a sample t, drawn randomly from a student's t-distribution with ν degrees of freedom, is greater than $t_{x(y),\nu}$ is $\frac{x}{y}$. That is, $P(t \sim t_\nu > t_{x(y),\nu}) = \frac{x}{y}$.

When the difference in population means is greater than or equal to δ, we say that one algorithm represents a *substantial* improvement over the other (see section 5.2). For $|\mu_d| < \delta$, choosing one system over another will have little effect on performance, so we are willing to accept an increased risk of a type-II error.

A reasonable value of δ must be determined for each case, taking into account the practical implications of a difference in means and how large this difference must be before it becomes meaningful.

We estimate σ_d by the sample standard deviation of the difference values obtained from robustness measurements on a small number n_s of images.

$$\sigma_d \approx \sqrt{\sum_{i=1}^{n_s} \frac{d_i - m_d}{n_s - 1}}. \tag{2}$$

Once the number of images n is calculated the full experiment can be performed, providing us with robustness data for n images.

5   Analysing the Data

The final stage of the comparison is the analysis of the robustness data. While the application of a hypothesis test (section 4.1) is a vital part of the framework, for a comparison to be fully sucessful the underlying assumptions must be verified and the results of the hypothesis test interpreted.

5.1   Testing Assumptions

To model the distribution of the sample data, a hypothesis test will make certain assumptions. These will vary depending on the specific test, but more powerful tests will typically require more stringent assumptions. Thus, in order to ensure a reliable comparison, all assumptions must be verified. If all assumptions hold then the test can be carried out as planned. If any of our assumptions are violated, the results of our planned test will be questionable. The same applies to any other assumptions made when designing the experiment, such as those required for the chosen robustness measurement (Sect. 3.2).

When an assumption is violated it may still be possible to follow the planned analysis provided the violation is mild and the test is known to be robust to that particular violation [25]. If such is not the case, then any assumption violations will require us to redesign the experiment so that the assumptions will be satisfied or choose an alternative hypothesis test with less stringent assumptions.

Paired t-test Assumptions. The paired t-test relies on three assumptions, each to be verified before the paired t-test can be applied.

A1 Pairing assumption: each a_i and b_i form a matched pair[8].
A2 Independence assumption: $a_i - b_i$ is independent of $a_j - b_j$
A3 Normality assumption: $d_i \sim N(\mu_d, \sigma)$

The sign test. Parametric tests assume the data have a specific distribution (the paired t-test assumes a normal distribution). When the distributional assumption is violated we need a non-parametric test, which does not rely on the data having any particular distribution. The *sign test* [26] is an alternative to the paired t-test, suitable for a non-normal, non-symmetric distribution. The null hypothesis for the sign test is that the median[9] of the paired differences is zero. If H0 holds, we expect $P(d_i > 0) = P(d_i < 0)$. Thus the test statistic t_s, formed by counting the number of positive and negative differences and taking the maximum,

$$t_s = \max(\#d_i > 0, \#d_i < 0)$$

is binomially distributed with trial sucess probability 0.5. The associated p-value is $p = 2 \times P(t \sim B(n, 0.5) \geq t_s)$.

5.2   Interpreting the Results

It is important to recall that hypothesis testing is a means to an end. Careful selection of the number of images and the application of an appropriate test is useful only so far as it allows meaningful comparison between algorithms.

---

[8] We use the term 'matched pair' to emphasise that the pair a_i, b_i cannot be arbitrarily assigned but must reflect a real dependency between a_i and b_i. This dependency typically arises because the measurements a_i and b_i are taken either from the same subject or from different subjects which have been matched so that they are are as similar as possible in the characteristics expected to influence the measurement.
[9] The sign test examines the *median* paired difference rather than the *mean* paired difference, however the median difference, like the mean, is still a good indicator of the general differences between schemes.

If the hypothesis test shows a significant difference exists, we should present its direction and size. The test results should be related back to the original problem so that we can state which (if any) system is better and indicate how much better it is.

When using statistical hypothesis testing there is a risk of placing too much focus on the statistical significance of the results. A *significant* difference exists when the observed difference does not appear to be due to chance (i.e. $p < \alpha$). A *substantial* difference exists when the observed difference is sufficiently large that it has a non-trivial impact on the system's performance in the intended application. While it is important to establish that the difference is significant, we are ultimately interested in the existence of a substantial difference.

Providing a 95% *confidence interval for the mean*[10] difference may be useful; if our minimum substantial difference δ^F is near the lower end of the confidence interval then the difference is probably substantial, if δ^F is near the upper end then the difference is more likely to be insubstantial.

Alternatively we can calculate an *effect size ES* that examines the mean difference relative to the pooled standard deviation of the sample values:

$$ES = \frac{m_d}{\sqrt{\frac{(n_a-1)s_a^2+(n_b-1)s_b^2}{n_a+n_b-2}}}.$$

The conventional values for effect size are small $ES = 0.2$, medium $ES = 0.5$ and large $ES = 0.8$.

Exactly what constitutes a *substantial* difference is both application dependent and subjective, good values for δ and ES can only be determined by careful consideration of the application domain.

6   Robustness Comparison for HVS and NoHVS

In this section we apply the concepts described in sections 3–5 to compare the robustness of the HVS and NoHVS algorithms to JPEG2000 resolution and quality compression (see sections 1.2 and 4). We need to choose a hypothesis test and determine the required number of images, source the images and generate the required robustness measurements, and finally test our assumptions, apply the hypothesis test and interpret our results.

6.1   Design

The experimental comparison begins with a design phase, in which the high level decisions required for data generation and analysis are made. This includes the choice of robustness measure, the selection of the hypothesis test and the calculation of how many images should be used.

---

[10] A 95% confidence interval for the mean μ_d^F is an interval centred at the estimated mean m which contains the true mean μ with probability .95.

Choose a Robustness Measure. We use the detection statistic as our robustness measure (Sect. 3.2). The detection statistic is chosen as a more efficient alternative to the true positive rate, particularly given both algorithms use the same detection statistic. While this will reduce the number of images required for our study, it will increase the effort required in the data interpretation step, as the detection statistic is a less direct measure of robustness than the true positive rate.

Select a suitable hypothesis test for the experiment. For each processing type F we use a paired t-test to decide between hypotheses $\mu_{\text{HVS}}^F = \mu_{\text{NoHVS}}^F$ and $\mu_{\text{HVS}}^F \neq \mu_{\text{NoHVS}}^F$ (Sect. 4). The paired t-test is chosen because it is a well-known and powerful test which exploits our ability to watermark identical copies of the same image to produce paired robustness measurements. To use a paired t-test we must verify three assumptions: pairing, independence and normality (Sect. 5.1).

The Pairing Assumption
> Measuring the robustness of both algorithms using the same set of test images $\mathcal{I}$ allows the formation of the required matched pairs a_i and b_i being the corresponding measurements of watermarking systems A and B from the same image (subject) $I_i \in \mathcal{I}$.

The Independence Assumption
> Both the image and the secret key influence the detection statistic, thus it is desirbable to use multiple keys in addition to multiple images. Using a separate pair a_{i_k}, b_{i_k} for each combination of image I_i and random seed k would result in pairs $\{a_{i_k}, b_{i_k} | 1 < k < n_k\}$ all sharing a dependency on I_i, violating the independence assumption.
>
> To resolve this problem, we use the average across the set of keys K. Averages are across keys rather than images because, for the algorithms we are using, changes in image cause more variation in the detection results than do changes in key. The average detection results a_i, b_i and a_j, b_j will be independent as they are taken from different subjects.

The Normality Assumption
> This is a distributional assumption, so its verification requires the data generation to be complete. Thus verification is left to Sect. 6.3.

Determine the required number of images. Our experiment will compare the robustness of algorithms HVS and NoHVS to two types of processing: quality compression $\mathcal{Q}$ and resolution compression $\mathcal{R}$. To obtain a concrete value for n, we must decide upon appropriate values for α, β and δ, and estimate the parameter σ_d (table 2).

Following convention, we choose $\alpha = 0.05$ and $\beta = 0.1$. For each processing type F we generate d_i^F values from 20 images to estimate σ_d^F.

The choice of δ^F is more subjective, we must find a value which represents a substantial practical difference between algorithms. We define a substantial difference in means as one which reduces the false negative error rate of the watermarking system by at least one third. We model the detection statistic as normally distributed, with mean $\mu_X^F \geq T$ and standard deviation $\sigma^F \approx \frac{\sigma_{\text{HVS}}^F + \sigma_{\text{NoHVS}}^F}{2}$

Table 2. Estimated standard deviation of difference values using a 20 image sample

F	σ_d^F
$\mathcal{R}$	0.00221
$\mathcal{Q}$	5.76

We calculate the false negative error rate for each algorithm at the watermark detection threshold $T = 6$ and find the difference in means δ^F which will result in a false negative rate reduction of at least 33% (table 3).

Table 3. Substantial difference in means δ

F	σ_{NoHVS}^F	σ_{HVS}^F	σ^F	δ^F
$\mathcal{R}$	2.43	2.43	2.43	0.992
$\mathcal{Q}$	5.08	4.91	5.00	2.23

This allows us to find the smallest value of n (table 4) which will satisfy equation (1). While in the resolution case our equation can be satisfied using only the minimum possible sample size of 2, in the quality case we require 62 images.

Table 4. Minimum number of images required to maintain error rates below α and β

F	α	β	n^F
$\mathcal{R}$	0.05	0.1	2
$\mathcal{Q}$	0.05	0.1	62

6.2 Data Generation

The data generation phase involves the establishment of image and key sets, the application of the watermarking algorithms and attacks and the gathering of the robustness measurements. There is some overlap between data generation and design; the decisions described here, such as the choice of imperceptibility measurement, should already have been considered in the design phase and calculating the required number of images, though included in design, requires that data generation be complete for a small number of images.

Establish the Image and Key Sets. We use $n = 62$ images from an online database of public domain images [27], they are natural colour images with horizontal and vertical dimensions ranging from 311 to 768; most have a mix of high and low frequency content with both smooth and textured regions. We use only $n_k = 10$ keys as there is relatively little variablity in the detection statistic for different keys.

Embed the Watermarks. For each system X, image I and key k we generate watermarked images $I'_{X,k}$. The watermarks are embedded using a modified version of the JasPer JPEG2000 implementation,[11] with the following options: $RGB \rightarrow YC_bC_R$ transform, 5-level DWT, Daubechies 9,7 filters, precinct size 128×128 and codeblock size 64×64. The compression rate is 0.999 for the full watermarked image with an intermediate quality layer at rate 0.01.

To achieve equal imperceptibility (Sect. 3.3) we use S-CIELAB, updated [28] to use CIEDE 2000 ΔE, which better approximates the human visual system. The settings used for S-CIELAB are those for a Dell 1702FP (Analog) monitor with 96dpi and viewed at a distance of 46cm. We define the distortion measure[12]

$$D_W(I'_{X,k}, I) = \text{99th percentile } \Delta E \text{ in S-CIELAB}(I'_{X,k}, I)$$

and set the threshold to $l_W = 4\Delta E$. The watermark strengths are adjusted so that $\forall I \in \mathcal{I}$, $X \in \{\text{HVS}, \text{NoHVS}\}$, $k \in \mathcal{K}$

$$|D_W(I'_{X,k}, I) - l_W| \leq 0.1$$

Process the Watermarked Images. Quality layers are discarded to produce the quality compressed images $I^{\mathcal{Q}}_{X,k}$ with $\frac{1}{100}$th the size in bytes of the original image. Resolution layers are discarded to produce the resolution compressed images $I^{\mathcal{R}}_{X,k}$ with $\frac{1}{256}$th the area of the original image.

Measure the Robustness. We use the detection statistic as our robustness measure (Sect. 3.2). For each processed image $I^F_{X,k}$ we obtain $\gamma(I^F_{X,k}, I, k)$ and average across keys to get $ds_X(I, F)$. For notational convenience we let I_i refer to the *ith* original image in our test set and use X^F_i to denote $ds_X(I_i, F)$.

The data are arranged into paired sets of measurements. The sets

$$\{\text{HVS}^{\mathcal{R}}_i\} \text{ and } \{\text{NoHVS}^{\mathcal{R}}_i\} \qquad 1 \leq i \leq n$$

describe the robustness of the HVS and NoHVS algorithms to resolution compression and the sets

$$\{\text{HVS}^{\mathcal{Q}}_i\} \text{ and } \{\text{NoHVS}^{\mathcal{Q}}_i\} \qquad 1 \leq i \leq n$$

describe the robustness of the HVS and NoHVS algorithms to quality compression. From these sets we produce the sets of paired differences $\{d^{\mathcal{R}}_i\}$ and $\{d^{\mathcal{Q}}_i\}$ required for our paired t-tests.

---

[11] The watermarking algorithms are designed to be applied during the compression process, immediately following the DWT transform step.

[12] S-CIELAB produces a ΔE distortion value for each pixel in the image. We use the 99th percentile (rather than the average) ΔE value because it is thought [29] to provide a closer match to subjective perceptability.

Table 5. Shapiro-Wilk Test for Normality of Paired Differences, $\alpha = 0.05$

F p	normal
$\mathcal{R}$ 4.82×10^{-6}	no
$\mathcal{Q}$ 0.484	yes

6.3   Analysis

The analysis phase begins once all the raw data have been generated. It involves the verification of any assumptions, application of the hypothesis test and interpretation of the results.

Test the Assumptions. We need to verify two sets of assumptions, the assumptions required by the hypothesis test and the assumptions required for using the means of our sample measurements for comparing the two algorithms.

We chose the *paired t-test* for our hypothesis test, for which two of the three assumptions, the pairing and independence assumptions (Sect. 5.1), were checked at the design stage. The remaining *normality assumption* must be verified at this stage.

To verify normality of the generated samples (paired differences d_i^F), we may use a hypothesis test for normality such as the Shapiro-Wilk test [30] (table 5), or a less formal (but arguably more effective) normal quantile plot[13] (Fig. 1). A p-value less than α, or a plot which deviates more than slightly from a straight $45°$ line, indicates non-normality.

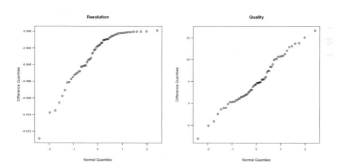

Fig. 1. Normal Quantile Plots of Paired Differences (Resolution and Quality)

Both techniques suggest a normal distribution in the quality case and a non-normal distribution in the resolution case. Thus for quality compression can proceed with the paired t-test as planned, but for resolution compression we need an

---

[13] A normal quantile plot matches the sorted sample values against the sorted values of a theoretical normal distribution such that if the values are normally distributed the points will form a straight line through the origin at a $45°$ angle. This allows us to visually identify deviations from normality by the comparing the plotted points to the ideal line.

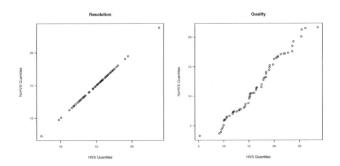

Fig. 2. Q-Q Plots of HVS against NoHVS (Resolution and Quality)

alternative *non-parametric* test, which does not require any particular distribution. We choose the sign test because the normal quantile plot for the resolution data indicates that the distribution of paired differences is non-symmetric.

In deciding to perform a comparison of means we assumed that the robustness values for our two algorithms had distributions with similar shape and spread (Sect. 4).

Similarity of shape can be checked using a quantile-quantile plot[14] (Fig. 2). In the quality case the distributions appear reasonably similar and for the resolution case there is a near-perfect match.

Similarity of spread can be checked by comparing the standard deviation of the samples. Both algorithms generate distributions with similar spread (table 6).

Table 6. Standard Deviation of Watermark Detection Statistic

x	σ^x_{NoHVS}	σ^x_{HVS}
$\mathcal{R}$	2.62	2.62
$\mathcal{Q}$	4.96	5.01

Perform the Hypothesis Test. The normality assumption was valid in the quality case and we apply the paired t-test (Sect. 4.1).

Table 7. Paired t-test for the quality compression

m_d	s_d	SE_d	t_d	p	$p < 0.05$
4.897	5.250	0.6667	7.345	5.907×10^{-10}	yes

In the resolution case, the assumption of normality was violated and we apply the sign test (Sect. 5.1).

---

[14] In a quantile quantile plot, the sorted samples from one algorithm are plotted against the sorted samples from the other algorithm. If the distributions have the same shape, then the points will form a straight line through the origin at a 45° angle.

Table 8. Sign test for resolution compression

$median_d$	t_s	p	$p < 0.05$
-0.00177	61	2.732×10^{-17}	yes

Interpret the Results. By interpreting the results we return our focus to the practical implications of the hypothesis test. We must consider which algorithm will perform better, by how much, and under what circumstances (Sect. 5.2). For both resolution and quality compression we consider both the size and direction of the mean robustness differences to determine whether the HVS algorithm represents a substantial improvement over the NoHVS algorithm. We estimate the missed detection rate to show the expected changes to the system performance when choosing one algorithm over the other.

The t-test results show there is a significant difference between HVS and No-HVS under quality compression. The difference in the mean similarity detection statistic for the two groups is 4.897. The effect size is 0.98 and a 95% confidence interval for the mean is (3.56, 6.23), well above $\delta^{\mathcal{Q}} = 2.23$. Thus we conclude that the HVS algorithm represents a substantial improvement in robustness to quality compression over the NoHVS algorithm.

Modeling the detection statistic for each algorithm using a normal distribution with mean and standard deviation estimates from our 62-image samples, we predict that choosing the HVS algorithm over the NoHVS algorithm would cause the rate of missed detections to drop from 13.6% to 1.96% (table 9).

Table 9. Estimated false negative rate for reduced quality images, T=6

X	$m_X^{\mathcal{Q}}$	$\sigma_X^{\mathcal{Q}}$	% False Negatives
HVS	11.4	5.01	1.96
NoHVS	16.3	4.96	13.6

The sign test results show a significant difference between HVS and NoHVS under resolution compression These differences are negative, indicating that the HVS algorithm is less robust than the NoHVS algorithm. However, these differences are very slight: the effect size is only 0.00107 and the 97% confidence interval for the median difference is (-0.00338, -0.00094), the minimum mean difference which we deemed substantial was $\delta^{\mathcal{R}} = 0.992$. Thus we conclude that there is not a substantial difference in robustness to resolution compression between the HVS and NoHVS algorithm.

Modeling the detection statistic for each algorithm using a normal distribution with mean and standard deviation estimates from our 62-image samples, we predict that choosing the HVS algorithm over the NoHVS algorithm would cause the rate of missed detections to rise from 0.0356% to 0.0357% (table 10).

Table 10. Estimated false negative rate for reduced resolution images, T=6

X	$m_X^{\mathcal{R}}$	$\sigma_X^{\mathcal{R}}$	% False Negatives
HVS	14.856	2.62	0.0357
NoHVS	14.853	2.62	0.0356

6.4   Conclusion

The HVS algorithm was designed to be robust to quality compression in addition to providing the same robustness to resolution compression as the NoHVS algorithm. This goal has largely been achieved; HVS shows a substantial increase in robustness to quality compression with a slight, but not substantial decrease in robustness to resolution compression.

Note that these experiments do not cover other forms of processing, so for applications involving other processing or using images with different characteristics from those in this experiment, additional testing would be required.

7   Concluding Remarks

Comparing watermarking algorithms and claiming superior performance is not straightforward. Claims that are made based on the results of experiments on only a handful of images cannot be relied upon. The most credible common practice is to run the algorithms on a 'large' set of images and and draw conclusions from the aggregate results. However there is no assurance that the size of set has been 'large enough', nor that any scientific method has been used to quantify the reliability of the results.

Our primary goal in this paper has been to demonstrate how one can determine the 'right' number of images for a comparison to achieve results with quantifiable reliability. Hypothesis testing and power analysis provide a formal and systematic approach to determining the number of sample images required to obtain reliable results. We focused on robustness comparison, using a case study comparing two spread-spectrum watermarking algorithms in terms of their robustness to scalable compression.

We aimed not only to provide an insight into the utility of hypothesis testing and power analysis for watermarking comparisons but also to examine them within the wider context of watermarking experiments. We explore the intricacies of watermarking comparison from the design of the experiment through to the interpretation of the results. We discuss issues that need to be carefully considered when performing a watermark comparison and the effects of design decisions on the outcome.

Noting that the field of watermarking relies largely on experiments for validation of performance claims, we believe our work will be of wide interest among practitioners in this field. We attempted to include the most relevant statistical tests for comparing our two watermarking algorithms, however the presented tests may not be the best choice for any given watermarking experiment and it is advisable to consult a statistician during the design phase.

The presented comparison used only two algorithms and two types of processing, if many algorithms or many processing types are examined it may be necessary to correct for increased probability of a type-I error, which will increase the number of images required to maintain the same error rates. Shaffer's paper [31] provides a good discussion of this problem and some of the available solutions.

The conclusions reached in a given comparison will only be applicable when the conditions of the experiments are a close match to the intended application for the watermarking system. Experiments using a single type of processing will be inadequate if we require robustness to many types of processing. Similarly, robustness tests against a wide range of processing types may not apply if only a few specific types of processing are expected.

The same applies to the types of images used. Because of this, comparison papers should outline not only the processing applied but also the composition of the test image set. The presented discussion assumes a random selection of images from a 'suitable' database. Such a database should either be representative of the target application domain, or contain images with the widest possible range of image properties of interest. (Image properties which will affect the robustness of a given algorithm may not be readily identifiable and may include the size, contrast, colour, texture, as well as whether they are natural or computer generated or belong to a specific domain such as medical images, cartoons or maps.) A more detailed description of 'suitable' would be a subject for other works.

A   Two Sample t-test

A two sample t-test is a standard way of comparing the means of two groups of independent samples $a_i | 1 \leq i \leq n_a$ and $b_j | 1 \leq j \leq n_b$. Both groups of samples are assumed to be drawn from normally distributed populations with the same standard deviation σ. The t-test tests against $H_0 : \mu_a = \mu_b$. The test statistic is the difference in sample means divided by the standard error for the estimate of the mean:

$$t_2 = \frac{m_a - m_b}{SE_{m_a - m_b}}$$

$$= \frac{m_a - m_b}{\sqrt{\frac{(n_a-1)s_a^2 + (n_b-1)s_b^2}{n_a+n_b-2}\left(\frac{1}{n_a} + \frac{1}{n_b}\right)}}$$

where s_a and s_b are the sample standard deviations from groups a and b respectively.

If H_0 is true this statistic will have a student's t distribution with $\nu = n_a + n_b - 2$ degrees of freedom, with an expected value of zero., the less it supports the null hypothesis.

The p-value is the probability p that a sample t drawn from a student's t distribution with ν degrees of freedom is further from zero than t_2.

$$p = 2 \times P(t \sim t_\nu > |t_2|) + P(t \sim t_\nu < -|t_2|).$$
$$= 2 \times P(t \sim t_\nu > |t_2|).$$

If $p < \alpha$, we reject H_0 with confidence $1 - \alpha$ and conclude that there is a significant difference in robustness between systems A and B.

B   HVS and NoHVS

B.1   NoHVS

Embedding

Input: I, k, N, ω_0
Output: I'
○ Use k to generate the pseudorandom sequence $W = (w_1, w_2, ..., w_N)$. W should have mean 0 and variance 1
○ Transform I using an L-level Daubechies 9,7 DWT
○ Set $I' = I$
○ Select coefficients $V = (v_1, v_2, ..., v_N)$ from I For each resolution level $R_j, j = 0, ..., L$ in I select $\{v \in R_j : v > \frac{2}{5} \max(v \in R)\}$ and place in V.
○ Select corresponding coefficients $V' = (v'_1, v'_2, ..., v'_N)$ from I'
○ Modify I' so that $v'_i = v_i(1 + \omega_0 w_i)$

Detection

Input: I^c, I, k, ω_0
Output: $\{True\}$ or $\{False\}$
○ Use k to generate $W = (w_1, w_2, ..., w_N)$ as for **Embedding**
○ Transform I as for **Embedding**
○ Transform I^c using an $(L - l)$-level Daubechies 9,7 discrete wavelet transform where l denotes the number of discarded resolution levels
○ Select $V = (v_1, v_2, ..., v_N)$ as for *Embedding*
○ Select corresponding coefficients $(v_1^c, v_2^c, ..., v_N^c)$ from I^c
○ Extract $W^c = (w_1^c, w_2^c, ..., w_N^c)$ where $w_i^c = \frac{1}{\omega_0}(\frac{v_i^c}{v_i} - 1)$
○ Calculate $\gamma(I^c, I, k) = sim(W^c, W) = \frac{W^c \cdot W}{\sqrt{W^c \cdot W^c}}$
○ If $\gamma(I^c, I, k) > T$ output $\{True\}$ else output $\{False\}$

B.2   HVS

The HVS algorithm is the same as the NoHVS except that the constant strength parameter ω_0 is replaced with a variable strength ω_i, which is adjusted by CSF$_i$

and Tex_i which represent the frequency and texture properties, respectively, of the coefficient v_i.

$$\omega_i = \omega_0 \text{CSF}_i \text{Tex}_i$$

Frequency. Let $c \in \{Y, Cb, Cr\}$ $r \in \{0, 1, ...N_L\}$ and $s = o_h o_v$, where $o_h, o_v \in \{L, H\}$, be the colour component, resolution level and subband orientation, respectively, for the coefficient v_i. Let f_{max} be the frequency in cycles per degree of visual angle of the full-resolution image at the target viewing distance.

The contrast sensitivity functions for the YC_b and C_r components we use are [32]

$$\text{CSF}_Y(f) = 0.997 f^2 e^{-0.970 f^{0.758}} + 0.221 e^{-0.800 f^{1.999}}$$
$$\text{CSF}_{Cb}(f) = e^{-0.2041 f^{0.900}}$$
$$\text{CSF}_{Cr}(f) = e^{-0.1521 f^{0.893}}$$

We also define f_{peak} as the frequency value which maximises $\text{CSF}_Y(f)$ and modify $\text{CSF}_Y(f)$ so that

$$\text{CSF}_Y(f) = 1 \qquad \forall f < f_{\text{peak}}$$

to allow for viewing distances further than the target viewing distance.

CSF

Input: $c, r, s = o_h o_v, f_{max}$
Output: CSF_i
$\circ\ l_r = 2^{(N_L - r)}$
$\circ\ f_h = \begin{cases} \frac{f_{max}}{4l_r} & \text{if } o_h = \text{L} \\ \frac{3 f_{max}}{4 l_r} & \text{if } o_h = \text{H} \end{cases}$
$\circ\ f_v = \begin{cases} \frac{f_{max}}{4 l_r} & \text{if } o_v = \text{L} \\ \frac{3 f_{max}}{l_r} & \text{if } o_v = \text{H} \end{cases}$
$\circ\ CSF_i = \frac{1}{CSF_c(f_h) CSF_c(f_v)}$

Texture. Let B_0 be an $n_b \times n_b$ block of coefficients centred at v_i, excluding those coefficients which are not within the subband boundary. The blocksize n_b should be small enough that any texture detected is reasonably local to the coefficient examined, yet sufficiently large to allow discrimination between textured and edged regions; we use $n_b = 17$.

Define blocks B_1 and B_2 similarly for the remaining two subbands at resolution r. Let S_j be the average coefficient magnitude of the subband containing block j and let $|B_j|$ be the number of coefficients in block j. [15] The threshold

---

[15] The number of coefficients $|B_j|$ in a given block may be less than the intended size of $n_b \times n_b$ if the block is too close to the subband boundary.

adjustment parameter q and the weights w_1 and w_2 are constants. The values $q = 0.\dot{6}$, $w_1 = 7.7\dot{2}$ and $w_2 = 0.4$ provide reasonable texture identification.

Texture

Input: $B_0, B_1, B_2, S_0, S_1, S_2$
Output: Tex_i
○ For j = 0 to 2 $$e(B_j) = \sum_{b \in B_j} \frac{|b|}{|B_j|}$$ $$c(B_j) = \sum_{b \in B_j \,\wedge\, |b| > qS_i} \frac{1}{|B_i|}$$
○ $E = \sqrt{\max(\ e(B_0)e(B_1),\ e(B_0)e(B_2),\ e(B_1)e(B_2)\ )}$
○ $C = \sqrt{\max(\ c(B_0)c(B_1),\ c(B_0)c(B_2),\ c(B_1)c(B_2)\ )}$
○ $t = w_1 C + w_2 E$
○ if $t < T_{\text{Tex}}$ set $t = 0$
○ $\text{Tex}_i = 1 + t$

Because texture occurs mainly at higher resolution levels while lower resolution levels tend to contain the important edge features, we set

$$Tex_i = 1 \qquad \text{whenever } v_i \in r \text{ s.t. } r < \lfloor \frac{N_l + 1}{3} \rfloor,$$

where $r \in \{0, 1, ..., N_l\}$ is the resolution level containing v_i.

References

1. Chen, T.P.C., Chen, T.: A framework for optimal blind watermark detection. In: ACM Multimedia 2001 Workshop on Multimedia and Security, Ottawa, Ontario, Canada (October 2001)
2. Mukherjee, D., Maitra, S., Acton, S.: Spatial domain digital watermarking of multimedia objects for buyer authentication. IEEE Transactions on Multimedia 6, 1–15 (February 2004)
3. Armeni, S., Christodoulakis, D., Kostopoulos, I., Stamatiou, Y., Xenos, M.: A transparent watermarking method for color images. In: First IEEE Balkan Conf. on Signal Processing, Communications, Circuits, and Systems, Istanbul, Turkey (June 2000)
4. Qiao, L., Cox, I.: Using perceptual models to improve fidelity and provide invariance to valumetric scaling for quantization index modulation watermarking. In: Proc. IEEE Int'l Conf. on Acoustics, Speech, and Signal Processing (ICASSP 2005), vol. 2, pp. 1–4 (March 2005)
5. Fridrich, J., Goljan, M.: Comparing robustness of watermarking techniques. In: Wong, P.W., Delp, E.J. (eds.) Security and Watermarking of Multimedia Contents, vol. 3657, pp. 214–225. SPIE, San Jose (January 1999)
6. Dittmann, J., Megías, D., Lang, A., Herrera-Joancomartí, J.: Theoretical framework for a practical evaluation and comparison of audio watermarking schemes in the triangle of robustness, transparency and capacity. In: Shi, Y.Q. (ed.) Transactions on Data Hiding and Multimedia Security I. LNCS, vol. 4300, pp. 1–40. Springer, Heidelberg (2006)

7. Kutter, M., Petitcolas, F.A.P.: A fair benchmark for image watermarking systems. In: Wong, P.W., Delp, E.J. (eds.) Security and Watermarking of Multimedia Contents, vol. 3657, pp. 226–239. SPIE, San Jose (January 1999)

8. Kim, H.C., Ogunley, H., Guitart, O., Delp, E.J.: The watermark evaluation testbed. In: Wong, P., Delp, E.J. (eds.) Proc. SPIE Int'l Conf. on Security and Watermarking of Multimedia Contents, San Jose, California, USA (January 2004)

9. ISO/IEC JTC 1/SC 29/WG 1: ISO/IEC FCD 15444-1: Information technology - jpeg2000 image coding system: Core coding system [WG 1 N 1646] (March 2000)

10. Su, J.K., Eggers, J.J., Girod, B.: Analysis of digital watermarks subjected to optimum linear filtering and additive noise. Signal Processing, Special Issue on Information Theoretic Issues in Digital Watermarking 8 (2001)

11. Adelsbach, A., Katzenbeisser, S., Sadeghi, A.-R.: A computational model for watermark robustness. In: Camenisch, J.L., Collberg, C.S., Johnson, N.F., Sallee, P. (eds.) IH 2006. LNCS, vol. 4437, pp. 145–160. Springer, Heidelberg (2007)

12. Pereira, S., Voloshynovskiy, S., Madueo, M., Marchand-Maillet, S., Pun, T.: Second generation benchmarking and application oriented evaluation. In: Moskowitz, I.S. (ed.) IH 2001. LNCS, vol. 2137, pp. 340–353. Springer, Heidelberg (2001)

13. Solachidis, V., Tefas, A., Nikolaidis, N., Tsekeridou, S., Nikolaidis, A., Pitas, I.: A benchmarking protocol for watermarking methods. In: Proc. IEEE International Conference on Image Processing, Thessaloniki, Greece, vol. 3, pp. 1023–1026 (October 2001)

14. Macq, B., Dittmann, J., Delp, E.: Benchmarking of image watermarking algorithms for digital rights management. Proc. of the IEEE 92(6), 971–984 (2004)

15. Kim, H.C., Delp, E.J.: A reliability engineering approach to digital watermark evaluation. In: Wong, P., Delp, E.J. (eds.) Proc. SPIE Int'l Conf. on Security and Watermarking of Multimedia Contents (January 2006)

16. Fridrich, J.: Combining low-frequency and spread spectrum watermarking. In: Proc. SPIE International Symposium on Optical Science, Engineering, and Instrumentation (1998)

17. Barni, M., Bartolini, F., Cappellini, V., Lippi, A., Piva, A.: A DWT-based technique for spatio-frequency masking of digital signatures. In: SPIE International Conf. on Security and Watermarking of Multimedia Contents, San Jose, CA, vol. 3657, pp. 31–39 (January 1999)

18. van Schyndel, R.G., Tirkel, A.Z., Osborne, C.F.: A digital watermark. In: International Conference on Image Processing, Austin, Texas, USA, vol. 2, pp. 86–90 (1994)

19. Bender, W., Gruhl, D., Morimoto, N., Lu, A.: Techniques for data hiding. IBM Systems Journal 35(3-4), 313–336 (1996)

20. Cox, I., Kilian, J., Leighton, T., Shamoon, T.: Secure spread spectrum watermarking for multimedia. IEEE Trans. Image Processing 6(12), 1673–1687 (1997)

21. Voloshynovskiy, S., Pereira, S., Iquise, V., Pun, T.: Attack modelling: Towards a second generation watermarking benchmark (2001) Signal Processing, Special Issue on Information Theoretic Issues in Digital Watermarking (2001)

22. Cox, I., Miller, M., Bloom, J.: Digital watermarking. Morgan Kaufmann Publishers Inc., San Francisco (2002)

23. Zhang, X., Wandell, B.: A spatial extension of CIELAB for digital color image reproduction. In: Proc. Soc. Inform. Display 1996 Digest, San Diego, pp. 731–734 (1996)

24. Bickel, P.J., Doksum, K.A.: 4. In: Mathematical Statistics: Basic Ideas and Selected Topics, Holden-Day, Inc., Oakland (1977)

25. Lee, W.: Experimental Design and Analysis. W. H. Freeman and Company, San Fransisco (1975)
26. Hollander, M., Wolfe, D.A.: Nonparametric Statistical Methods. John Wiley & Sons, Inc., New York (1973)
27. The gimp-savvy photo archive, http://gimp-savvy.com/PHOTO-ARCHIVE/index.html (last access: 5 May 2005)
28. Sharma, G., Wu, W., Dalal, E.: The CIEDE2000 color-difference formula: Implementation notes, supplementary test data, and mathematical observations. Color Research and Application 30(1), 21–30 (2005)
29. Morovic, J., Sun, P.: Visual differences in colour reproduction and their colorimetric correlates. In: IS&T/SID 10th Color Imaging Conference, pp. 292–297 (2002)
30. Shapiro, S.S., Wilk, M.: An analysis of variance test for normality (complete samples). Biometrika 52(3/4), 591–611 (1965)
31. Shaffer, J.P.: Multiple hypothesis testing. Annual Review of Psychology 46, 561–576 (1995)
32. Nadenau, M.J.: Integration of Human Colour Vision Models into High Quality Image Compression. PhD thesis, Ecole Polytechnique Federale de Lausanne, Switzerland (2000)

A Desynchronization Resilient Watermarking Scheme

Xiaojun Qi and Ji Qi

Department of Computer Science, Utah State University, Logan, UT 84322-4205
Xiaojun.Qi@usu.edu, jiqi79@gmail.com

Abstract. This paper presents a content-based desynchronization resistant digital image watermarking scheme. The image content is represented by strong important feature points obtained by our robust and improved Harris corner detector. These feature points are more resistant to geometric attacks and are therefore used by the Delaunay triangle matching and image restoration method to reduce synchronization errors. The spread-spectrum-based blind watermark embedding and retrieval scheme is applied in the Fourier domain of each perceptually highly textured subimage. The multiplicative scheme is then used to embed the same copy of the watermark at highly secure mid-frequency positions generated by one-way hash functions with different secret keys. The watermark detection decision is based on the number of matched bits between the recovered and embedded watermarks in embedding subimages. Experimental results demonstrate that our scheme is more robust to desynchronization attacks (i.e., geometric and common image processing attacks) than other peer feature-based approaches.

Keywords: Desynchronization resilient digital watermarking, important feature points, spread-spectrum-based blind watermarking, Delaunay triangle matching.

1 Introduction

With the rapid growth of multimedia data distribution, many digital watermarking schemes have been proposed for copyright protection. The robustness of the watermark to common image processing and geometric attacks is essential in many applications [1]. However, these desynchronization attacks are difficult to tackle due to induced synchronization errors in watermark detection and decoding. Several watermarking schemes, including template-based, invariant-domain-based, moment-based, and feature-based, have been developed to counterattack desynchronization distortions.

Template-based watermarking algorithms [2], [3], [4] embed image independent templates to assist synchronization in watermark detection process. However, these template features can be exploited [5] to destroy the synchronization pattern. Invariant-domain-based watermarking algorithms [6], [7], [8], [9] generally provide a RST (Rotation, Scaling, and Translation) invariant domain to maintain synchronization under affine transforms. The Fourier-Mellin transform and log-polar resampling are two typical examples. However, the interpolation accuracy and aliasing in the resampling and integration may cause problems in synchronization. Moment-based watermarking

Y.Q. Shi (Ed.): Transactions on DHMS IV, LNCS 5510, pp. 29–48, 2009.

algorithms utilize ordinary geometric moments [10], [11], [12] or Zernike moments [13], [14] to solve the geometric invariance problem. However, perfect invariance cannot be achieved due to the discretization errors. Feature-based watermarking algorithms [15], [16], [17], [18], [19], [20] use image dependent feature points to represent invariant reference points for both embedding and detection. They generally are the best approaches to resisting desynchronization distortions since feature points provide stable references for both watermark embedding and detection. Several related, representative schemes are briefly reviewed here.

Bas *et al.* [15] used the Harris corner detector for feature extraction. These feature points were mixed with a Delaunay tessellation to mark each triangle for embedding the watermark. The original watermark triangles were then warped during the detection to correlate with the corresponding marked triangles. Similarly, Seo and Yoo [16], [17] extracted feature points using the Harris-Laplace detector and decomposed the image into disjointed local circular or elliptical regions for watermark embedding and extraction. Lee *et al.* [18] proposed to use the SIFT (Scale-Invariant Feature Transform) to determine the local circular regions for watermarking. The simulation results from all of the above methods show that the robustness of each scheme depends on the capacity for preserving feature points after geometric transformation, especially on images with more texture and images with less texture and large homogeneous areas. Moreover, these methods embed the watermark in the spatial domain after geometric normalization according to the shapes of the region. Consequently, watermark robustness to common image processing is not satisfactory and the feature points-based transformation domain watermarking schemes were proposed. Tang and Hang [19] adopted the Mexican hat wavelet scale interaction method to extract feature points. They embedded and extracted the watermark in the normalized disks centered at the extracted feature points. Wang *et al.* [20] improved Tang's method by using the scale invariant Harris-Laplace detector to find the radius of each circular region. However, Tang's scheme performs well under only mild geometric distortion and certain common image processing attacks. The watermark capacity of both schemes is only 16 bits, which may restrict their practical applications.

In this paper, we develop a desynchronization resilient watermarking scheme. This scheme combines the advantages of important feature extraction, perceptual analysis, one-way hash functions, and spread-spectrum-based blind watermark embedding and retrieval to reduce the watermark synchronization problem and resist different attacks. Section 2 describes the proposed robust feature extraction method. Section 3 briefly presents our variants of two important techniques used in the proposed scheme. Section 4 covers the details of the watermark embedding and detection procedure. Section 5 compares our scheme with three feature-based approaches in terms of robustness against both geometric distortions and common image processing attacks. In addition, we also demonstrate the performance of our proposed scheme on 105 images of various textures under different Stirmark attacks. Section 6 concludes this presentation.

2   Feature Points Extraction

Extracting feature points is the most important step in the proposed digital image watermarking scheme. In order to detect watermarks without access to the original images, we look for feature points that are perceptually significant and can thus resist various types of desynchronization distortions. These image-content-bounded feature points can be further used as synchronization markers (i.e., anchor points) in watermark detection. To this end, we propose a robust and improved Harris corner detector to find relatively strong IFPs (Important Feature Points) to reduce the synchronization errors in watermark detection. Our two major contributions are:

- Improve the Harris corner detector [21] to reduce noise effect and regulate the density of IFPs based on the dimension and texture of the image.
- Strengthen the improved Harris corner detector to discard some non-stable IFPs.

These two improvements can also be applied to other detectors to achieve better performance.

The algorithmic flow of our improved Harris corner detector is summarized as follows:

1. Apply a rotationally symmetric 3×3 Gaussian low-pass filter with the standard deviation of 0.5 to blur the original image to increase the noise resistance.
2. Compute three derivative images, A, B, and C, by convolving the blurred image with the horizontal, vertical, and diagonal edge filters, respectively.
3. Apply the same Gaussian low-pass filter to blur three derivative images (e.g., A, B, and C) to further increase the noise tolerance.
4. Calculate the corner response function R as defined in [21], i.e., $R = (AB-C)^2 - 0.4(A+B)^2$, within a circular window, which is at the image center and covers the largest area of the original image. The resulting function reduces the effect of image center based rotation attacks and removes the corner points near the image border.
5. Search for IFPs whose corner response value $R(x,y)$'s are larger than a threshold T and are the local maxima within a circular neighborhood centered at (x, y).

We choose the circular neighborhood window to avoid the increasing detector anisotropy and to obtain a homogeneous distribution of feature points in the image. It is also important to determine the appropriate window size since a small window makes the feature points concentrate on textured areas and a large window tends to isolate the feature points. Fig. 1 illustrates the effect of different window sizes on the resultant feature points. We can easily observe that the smaller window yields more feature points. However, these "extra" feature points will require more computational cost in the detection process. The larger window yields fewer feature points and requires fewer computational cost in the detection process. However, the possibility of losing some IFPs is also increased. In order to make a compromise between the number of feature points and the computational cost in watermark detection, we determine a suitable window size based on the dimension and texture of the image. We roughly classify image textures as high, medium, and low, based on the ratio of the feature points to the total number of pixels in an image, wherein the feature points are obtained by using our improved Harris corner detector with a fixed 3×3 neighborhood window. That is:

$$\text{image has}\begin{cases} \text{high texture} & \text{if ratio} \geq 0.01 \\ \text{medium texture} & \text{if ratio} \geq 0.002 \\ \text{low texture} & \text{if ratio} \geq 0.0001 \end{cases} \tag{1}$$

The diameter of the circular window is calculated:

$$D = \frac{\sqrt{wh}}{np} \tag{2}$$

where integers w and h respectively represent the width and height of the image; integer p is an empirical value (i.e., $p = 5$) for obtaining a reasonable number of feature points for images with large homogeneous areas; and integer n is the window size quantizer, which depends on the texture of the image. It is set to be 2, 2.5, and 3 for images with high, medium, and low textures, respectively.

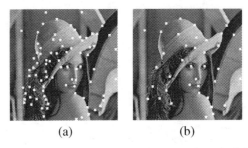

(a)   (b)

Fig. 1. The effect of different window sizes on the feature points. (a) 26×26. (b) 52×52.

Our improved Harris corner detector ensures to extract IFPs in a noisy image. However, these IFPs may not be robust under certain geometric or common image processing attacks. Fig. 2 demonstrates this observation by displaying the IFPs of two attacked Lena images. We can clearly see that some IFPs are present in both attacked images while others are only present in one attacked image.

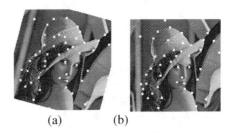

(a)   (b)

Fig. 2. The non-robustness of IFPs under attacks. (a) IFPs after rotation. (b) IFPs after resizing.

In order to keep the strong IFPs which resist geometric attacks, we further enhance the improved Harris detector by quantitatively evaluating its capacity for preserving the IFPs when the image undergoes certain attacks. This evaluation function is computed as:

$$Score = \frac{Num_{kept} - (Num_{new} + Num_{loss})}{Num_{kept} + Num_{loss}} = \frac{Num_{kept} - (Num_{new} + Num_{loss})}{Num_{ori}} \tag{3}$$

where Num_{ori} denotes the number of IFPs present in the original image; Num_{new}, Num_{loss}, and Num_{kept} represent the number of IFPs that have been created, destroyed, and preserved after certain attacks, respectively. The preservation, creation, or loss status of these feature points is evaluated by performing an inverse transformation, which restores the attacked image to be aligned with the original image, on the IFPs obtained from the attacked image. This evaluation function yields the maximal value of 1 when the detector precisely finds the IFPs under a certain attack, i.e., $Num_{new} = Num_{loss} = 0$. In general, the larger the *Score*, the more capacity of the detector to preserve the IFPs under attacks.

Fig. 3 illustrates the block diagram of finding the relatively strong IFPs. Various image rotation and scaling attacks have been performed on the original image to find several attacks that preserve most of the strong IFPs in the original image. Our extensive experimental results show that random attacks can roughly estimate all possible rotations and scaling factors. The best attacks that achieve the highest *Score* values will be further used to individually pre-attack the original image to find the IFPs in its corresponding attacked images. Choosing these pre-attacks ensures that a decent number of strong IFPs can be obtained to reduce the synchronization errors. The strong IFPs are obtained by:

$$IFP_{strong} = IFP_{ori} \bigcap_{i=1}^{n} \{Align(IFP_{Attack_i})\} \tag{4}$$

where IFP_{ori} represents the IFPs in the original image; IFP_{Attack_i} represents the IFPs after the *i*th best attack, which can be either a rotation or a scaling attack; and $Align(\bullet)$ is an alignment operator to register the original and attacked images; and n is the number of the best attacks and is adaptively chosen based on the image texture. In our system, we set n to be 6 for high textured images, 4 for medium textured images, and 2 for low textured images.

Fig. 4 illustrates the effect of different pre-attacks on the resulting IFPs and shows the relatively strong IFPs obtained by intersecting IFPs of the original and its pre-attacked images. We can easily observe the sensitivity of the IFPs to different attacks. That is, some IFPs may disappear or show up or shift a bit after attacks. Consequently, it is impossible to locate the robust IFPs which can survive various attacks in the real world. To address this challenging issue, we select a few best pre-attacks to extract the strong IFPs that are likely preserved under different attacks. Such a choice keeps the balance between the robustness and the number of strong IFPs. Specifically, the intersection operation increases the robustness of the extracted strong IFPs and keeps enough IFPs to regain the synchronization (i.e., align the watermarked image with the original image). In other words, a robust resynchronization can be achieved by using a few best pre-attacks for a compromise between the robustness and the number of strong IFPs. The rationale for choosing the best pre-attacks is based on the following observations:

1. Most IFPs surviving a rotation or scaling attack can survive any combined RST attacks or any image processing attacks if the image is not cropped. The following intuitive proofs support this observation: a) Cropping may result in substantial loss of the IFPs and therefore will not be considered as a pre-attack. b) A feature point,

major characteristic in an image, must be differentiated from its neighbors no matter what kinds of the attacks are performed on the image. c) Any rotation or scaling attack, like any combined RST attack, requires an interpolation operation to modify the intensity of each pixel. The image processing attacks will modify the intensity of each pixel in another way. However, these modifications should not make the differentiation between the feature point and its neighbors disappear. That is, most feature points should still stand out when compared to their neighbors after geometric and image processing attacks. As a result, we can always use a rotation or scaling attack to find potential IFPs.

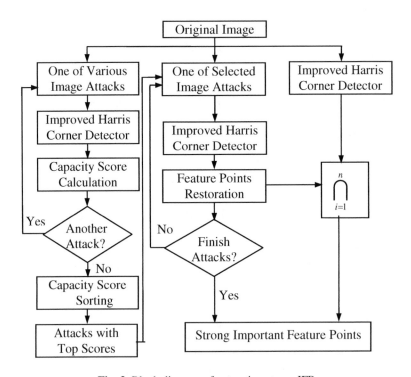

Fig. 3. Block diagram of extracting strong IFPs

2. The IFPs which are preserved after several pre-attacks are more robust against attacks than the other IFPs which are destroyed or created after the pre-attacks.
3. The best pre-attacks usually yield more IFPs than any other pre-attacks (e.g., random attacks, worst attacks, or image processing attacks). This leads to more anchor points for synchronization and therefore increases the possibilities for finding the geometric transformation in watermark detection.
4. The IFPs obtained from the best pre-attacks always intersect with majority IFPs obtained from an attacked image. This indicates that we can always find enough IFPs to perform synchronization.

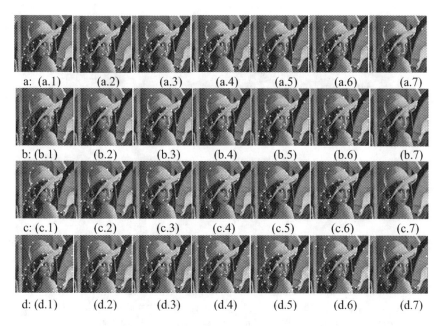

a: (a.1)   (a.2)   (a.3)   (a.4)   (a.5)   (a.6)   (a.7)

b: (b.1)   (b.2)   (b.3)   (b.4)   (b.5)   (b.6)   (b.7)

c: (c.1)   (c.2)   (c.3)   (c.4)   (c.5)   (c.6)   (c.7)

d: (d.1)   (d.2)   (d.3)   (d.4)   (d.5)   (d.6)   (d.7)

Fig. 4. The effect of different pre-attacks on the resultant strong IFPs. (a) IFPs obtained from 6 best pre-attacks. (a.1) R180° (a.2) R250° (a.3) R265° (a.4) R280° (a.5) R60° (a.6) S0.95 (a.7) Final strong IFPs by intersecting the original and its 6 best pre-attacked images. (b) IFPs obtained from 6 worst pre-attacks. (b.1) R145° (b.2) R235° (b.3) R220° (b.4) R320° (b.5) R190° (b.6) S0.90 (b.7) Final strong IFPs by intersecting the original and its 6 worst pre-attacked images. (c) IFPs obtained from 6 random pre-attacks. (c.1) R16° (c.2) R145° + S0.95 (c.3) R240° + S0.87 (c.4) R110° + S0.96 + T[5, 5] (c.5) R68° + S0.85 + T[10, 10] (c.6) S0.8 +T[10, 10] (c.7) Final strong IFPs by intersecting the original and its 6 random pre-attacked images. (d) IFPs obtained from 6 common image processing pre-attacks. (d.1) Median filtering 2×2 (d.2) Median filtering 3×3 (d.3) Mean filtering 3×3 + JPEG90% (d.4) Sharpening (d.5) Gaussian filtering (d.6) Histogram equalization (d.7) Final strong IFPs after intersecting the original and its 6 common image processing pre-attacked images. Here, R denotes rotation, S denotes scaling, and T denotes translation.

5. The IFPs obtained from the worst pre-attacks seem to be the most stable ones. However, some IFP may not be preserved under certain attacks due to the sensitivity of the IFPs to different attacks. In addition, these IFPs may not possess sufficient anchor points for the synchronization in the detection process.

Fig. 5 demonstrates the final preserved strong IFPs by applying our proposed robust and improved Harris corner detector on four images with different textures. That is, random rotation and scaling operations are respectively applied on each image to find its best pre-attacks. The improved Harris detector is then applied to find the IFPs for each original image and its corresponding best pre-attacked images. The intersection of all IFPs yields strong IFPs to be saved for the detection process. As shown in Fig. 5, the proposed approach effectively eliminates some unreliable feature points which fail to be detected after certain geometric attacks.

Fig. 5. Relatively strong and important feature points

3   Our Variants of Related Techniques

3.1   The PN-Sequence and One-Way Hash Functions

We use the PN (Pseudo-Noise) sequence based spread spectrum method in our system due to its robustness against noise and its capability to achieve error free transmission near or at the limits set by Shannon's noisy channel coding theorem [22]. This sequence combined with the watermark is adaptively embedded into mid-frequency positions in the DFT domain since high-frequency watermark can be easily eliminated by lossy compression and low-frequency watermark is usually noticeable.

We improve the one-way hash function [23], which is easy to compute and difficult to invert, to generate the highly secure mid-frequency positions by the following seven steps:

1. Save all middle frequency positions into vector V.
2. Randomly choose two large prime numbers p and q, and compute the secret key $n=pq$.
3. Obtain two seeds X and Y using the encipher process :

$$X = m^K \bmod n; \ Y = X^2 \bmod n; \tag{5}$$

   where m is the original image identification number (i.e., a numerical serial number for registering the image) and K is the second secret key.
4. Calculate an index l by:

$$Y = Y^2 \bmod n \ ; l = (Y \bmod n) \bmod length(V) \ ; \tag{6}$$

5. Choose the lth item in V as the embedding position.
6. Remove the lth item from V so no duplicated positions are produced and no collision occurs.
7. Repeat steps 4-6 until the total number of embedding positions is reached.

These highly secure embedding positions can be easily reproduced given the same secret keys n and K. In the meantime, the reproduction of these positions is computationally infeasible without knowing n and K. To ensure the attackers cannot find out the watermark embedding positions by comparing several watermarked copies, different secret keys are used to generate embedding positions for each embedding subimage.

3.2 Blind Embedding and Retrieval

A watermarking system should be secure and reliable. It is also desirable to extract the watermark independent of the original image. In our system, we adopt the blind retrieval scheme of MPEG video watermark [24], [25] to eliminate the need of storing values at embedding positions of each host subimage. We employ this blind retrieval scheme in the DFT domain instead of their proposed DCT domain. The multiplicative instead of additive embedding is also applied in our modified scheme. That is:

$$F\hat{I}_i = FI_i + FI_i \times G \times W_i \times p_i, \quad i = 1,...,N \qquad (7)$$

where FI_i is the original mid-frequency DFT sequence with length N, $F\hat{I}_i$ is the watermarked DFT sequence, G is the embedding strength, p_i is the bipolar PN sequence generated by a secret key, and W_i is the blind watermark bit sequence obtained by repeating the bipolar watermark message w_i by a spreading factor s such that $W_i = w_j$ for $js \leq i < (j+1)s$.

The blind retrieval can be achieved by de-spreading the blind watermarked bit sequence using the correlation detector. The same embedding PN-sequence p_i is used to multiply the possibly watermarked sequence:

$$W_i' = p_i F\hat{I}_i \qquad (8)$$

The W_i' is further grouped into blocks of size s where each block is computed:

$$\sum_{i=js+1}^{(j+1)s} p_i F\hat{I}_i = \underbrace{\sum_{i=js+1}^{(j+1)s} p_i FI_i}_{S1} + \underbrace{G \sum_{i=js+1}^{(j+1)s} p_i^2 FI_i W_i}_{S2} \qquad (9)$$

where $j = 0,...,n-1$ and n is the length of w_i. For a large s, FI_i is statistically uncorrelated with p_i. As a result, $S_2 \gg S_1$ and Eq. (9) is simplified:

$$\sum_{i=js+1}^{(j+1)s} p_i F\hat{I}_i \approx \underbrace{G \sum_{i=js+1}^{(j+1)s} p_i^2 FI_i W_i}_{S2} = \underbrace{G \sum_{i=js+1}^{(j+1)s} FI_i W_i}_{S2} \qquad (10)$$

Since FI_i and G are positive, the embedded bipolar watermark bit w_j is therefore similar to the sign of the correlation sum $\hat{w}_j$. That is:

$$w_j \approx \hat{w}_j = sign\left(\sum_{i=js+1}^{(j+1)s} p_i F\hat{I}_i\right), \quad j = 0,...,n\text{-}1 \qquad (11)$$

4 Watermark Embedding and Detection Scheme

4.1 Watermark Embedding Scheme

Our watermark is designed for copyright protection. We view all possible embedding subimages as independent communication channels. To improve the robustness of the transmitted watermark bits, all channels carry the same copy of the chosen water-mark. During the detection process, we claim the existence of watermark if one copy of the embedded watermark is correctly detected in one embedding subimage. The watermark embedding process is detailed step by step as follows:

1. **Image tessellation:** Evenly divide the 8-bit grayscale image into 3×3 nonoverlap-ping subimages. The last several nondivisible rows and columns are not used for embedding.
2. **Perceptual analysis:** Apply the Harris corner detector to find all feature points in the original image by using a 3×3 window. Choose the subimages that have a large number of feature points to be embedding blocks. These blocks are perceptually high textured.
3. For each perceptually high textured subimage $SubA$:
    3.1 **DFT:** Apply global DFT to obtain $FSubA$.
    3.2 **Position Generator:** Generate highly secure embedding positions in the mid-frequencies between f_1 and f_2 in the upper half plane of $FSubA$ by using our one-way hash function.
    3.3 $\oplus$ **operation:** Embed the spread bipolar watermark message bit W_j into each position (x_k, y_k) by using the multiplicative formula [26]:

$$FSubA(x_k, y_k)' = FSubA(x_k, y_k) + FSubA(x_k, y_k) \times G \times W_j \times p_j \qquad (12)$$

where $p_j \in \{1, -1\}$ (zero mean and unit variance) is the PN-sequence generated by a secret key. The same changes are carried out at center-based symmetric positions due to the constraints in the DFT domain for obtaining a real image.
    3.4 **IDFT (Inverse DFT):** Apply the IDFT to $FSubA'$ to obtain the watermark em-bedded subimage $SubA'$, which replaces the original subimage $SubA$.

The proposed robust and improved Harris detector is finally used to find strong IFPs in the watermarked image. The position of each strong IFP, the bipolar water-mark message bit sequence W_i, the number of embedding positions Len, two secret keys n and K for our one-way hash function in each subimage, two middle frequency ratios, and the secret key for generating the PN-sequence are saved for watermark de-tection. Since strong IFPs are obtained via the intersection operation, the number of IFPs is optimized and the storage is minimal compared to the cost of saving the image itself. If all the information is compressed, the storage cost will be further minimized.

4.2 Watermark Detection Scheme

The watermark detection procedure does not need the original image. The relatively strong IFPs are first extracted by intersecting the IFPs obtained by applying our pro-posed improved Harris corner detector on the probe image and a few randomly rotated probe images. Two sets of Delaunay tessellation-based triangles [27] are gen-erated using the strong IFPs found in the probe image and the saved strong IFPs, re-spectively. These two sets of triangles are then matched to determine the possible geometric transformations the probe image has undergone. These geometric transfor-mations are further utilized to restore the probe image so synchronization errors are minimized in the detection.

The choice of Delaunay tessellation is based on two attractive properties: 1) Local property: If a vertex disappears, the tessellation is only modified on connected triangles. 2) Stability area: Each vertex is associated with a stability area where the tessellation pattern is not changed when the vertex is moved within this area. That is, the tessellation patterns of other triangles remain the same even though losing or shifting an IFP affects the triangle(s) connected to it. In addition, two properties of the Delaunay tessellation always ensure that an identical generation of triangles can be obtained if the relative positions of the IFPs do not change. We implemented the Qhull algorithm [28] to generate the IFPs-based triangles due to its fast speed and less memory constraints.

In our system, the angle radians are used to match Delaunay tessellation-based triangles. That is, if two triangles have very similar angle radians (i.e., the angle difference is less than 0.01 radian), they are claimed to be likely matched. The possible geometric transformations are determined from the matched triangle pairs since the IFPs-based triangles undergo the same transformation as the image itself. The detailed steps are:

1. Calculate the scaling factor SF by resizing the probe triangle to the same size as the target matched triangle.
2. Calculate the translation factor TF by registering one of the vertices of the matched triangle pair.
3. Calculate the rotation factor RF by aligning the other two unregistered vertices of the matched triangle pair.

These factors form a 3-element tuple (SF, TF, RF) where SF measures the scaling ratio up to a precision of 1/10, TF measures the translation in pixel numbers, and RF measures the rotation angle in an integer degree.

Since an image and the within triangles undergo exactly the same transformation, we use the majority of the identical 3-element tuples obtained from all matched triangle pairs to restore the probe image. The same embedding procedure is applied to the restored probe image to obtain the watermark embedded DFT sequence $FSubA_i''$ for each potential embedding subimage i. The blind watermark retrieval scheme is then applied to extract the bipolar watermark bit sequence W_j', which is compared with the original watermark bit sequence W_j to determine the presence of the watermark. That is, the number of matched bits in a potential embedding subimage is compared with a threshold to determine whether the watermark is present in the probe image. This threshold is calculated based on the false-alarm probability that may occur in watermark detection. The Bernoulli trails are used to model W_j' since every watermark bit is an independent random variable. The probability of a k-bit match between extracted and original watermark bit sequences with a length of n is calculated as:

$$p_k = \binom{n}{k} \cdot p^k (1-p)^{n-k} \tag{13}$$

where p is the success probability for the extracted bit to be matched with the original watermark bit. We further simplify Eq. (13) by assuming p to be 1/2:

$$p_k = \left(\frac{1}{2}\right)^n \cdot \left(\frac{n!}{k!(n-k)!}\right) \tag{14}$$

The false-alarm probability for each embedding subimage is a cumulative probability of the cases that $k_i \geq T_i$, where k_i and T_i respectively represent the number of matching bits and the threshold for each subimage i. It is computed as:

$$P_{false-alarm}(i) = \sum_{k_i=T_i}^{n} \left(\frac{1}{2}\right)^n \cdot \left(\frac{n!}{k_i!(n-k_i)!}\right) \tag{15}$$

Based on Eq. (15), the perfect match between the extracted and original watermarks in a single embedding subimage leads to a false alarm probability of 6.10×10^{-5}. This is a low false alarm probability so we can confidently claim the watermark exists. In our system, we will check the perfect match in any embedding subimage to indicate the presence of the watermark.

5   Experimental Results

To evaluate the performance of the proposed watermarking scheme, we conducted experiments on various standard 8-bit grayscale images and different kinds of attempting attacks. We first perform the watermark invisibility test using four 512×512 8-bit gray-level images. We then illustrate the effectiveness of the proposed strong IFPs-based image restoration scheme, which functions as a self-synchronization scheme to align the possibly geometrically distorted watermarked image with the original one. Next, we perform extensive comparisons with three well designed feature-based RST resilient watermarking schemes proposed by Tang and Hang [19], Wang et al. [20], and Bas et al. [15]. Finally, we summarize the performance of our proposed scheme under a variety of Stirmark attacks on 105 8-bit watermarked grayscale images.

5.1   Watermark Invisibility Test

We evaluate watermark invisibility on four images: Lena, Pepper, Airplane, and Baboon. These four images correspond to several texture categories. For example, Baboon includes textured areas with high frequency components; Lena and Airplane include large homogeneous areas whereas Lena has sharp edges; and Pepper falls in a low-textured category. The PSNRs of these four watermarked images are 43.33, 44.06, 42.27, and 37.62, respectively. These PSNR values are all greater than 35.00db, which is the empirical value for the image without any perceivable degradation [29].

5.2   Important Restoration Test

Image restoration is an important step in the proposed watermarking scheme. In general, we apply the Delaunay tessellation on the strong IFPs to generate triangles, and use angle degrees to find the matched triangles between the original and probe images. We further use these matched triangles to find the possible geometric attacks. Table 1 lists four image texture dependent parameters and the number of strong IFPs determined by applying our image-texture-based improved and robust Harris corner detector on four images with different textures. These four parameters are *Ratio* (the factor for classifying image textures), *Type* (the texture decided by Eq. (1)), *D* (the diameter of the circular window of the robust and improved Harris corner detector), and *SNum* (the number of embedding subimages determined by perceptual analysis). It clearly shows that diameter *D* is determined by the image texture. That is, the more complicate the texture, the larger the diameter *D*. The value of *SNum* indicates the distribution of the perceptually high texture within an image. These adaptive parameters are automatically determined based on image textures. They improve the accuracy in finding the image-content-based strong IFPs and the robustness in resisting geometric and common image processing attacks on different textured images. We also observe that the number of IFPs is less than 35 for all the test images with different textures. This observation clearly demonstrates that our improved and robust Harris corner detector does regulate the number of IFPs. It also indicates that the cost of saving IFPs for watermark synchronization is minimal compared with the cost of saving the host image.

Table 1 also lists the ratios between the number of matched triangle pairs for determining the geometric transformation and the total number of matched triangle pairs under four random geometric attacks. All simulation results yield ratios of larger than 85%, which indicate a high accuracy in finding the possible geometric transformation a probe image may undergo. When comparing the results between the images, it should be noted that the number of matched triangle pairs is not linearly related to the number of strong IFPs due to the sensitivity of the IFPs to different attacks. However, our improved and robust Harris corner detector generates relatively strong IFPs to reduce the synchronization errors. In addition, two properties of the Delaunay tessellation always ensure that there are enough matched triangles, as indicated by high ratios in Table 1, for restoring the probe image.

Table 1. Image adaptive parameters and ratios under different attacks

Images	Images Adaptive Parameters				Robust IFPs	Geometric Attacks			
	Ratio	Type	D	SNum		(a)	(b)	(c)	(d)
Lena	0.002	Med	41	3	27	15/16	23/25	10/11	15/16
Baboon	0.01	High	51	9	33	18/20	25/27	12/14	12/12
Pepper	0.0013	Low	34	4	25	21/22	17/18	13/15	16/17
Plane	0.0033	Med	41	6	28	17/18	24/26	10/10	15/16

5.3 Comparison with Feature-Based RST Robust Watermarking Schemes

We compare the proposed scheme with three feature-based RST robust watermarking schemes, namely Tang's scheme [19], Wang's scheme [20], and Bas's scheme [15] in Tables 2 through 4. Each gray cell indicates that the corresponding method fails to detect the watermark under the corresponding distortion. Table 2 summarizes the detection results compared with the schemes of Tang [19] and Wang [20] against common image processing attacks. Table 3 summarizes the detection results compared with the schemes of Tang [19] and Wang [20] against desynchronization attacks. These two tables show the ratio between the number of correctly detected watermarked embedding regions and the number of original embedded watermarked embedding regions. Here, we use the term "detection rate" to denote it. Similarly, the detection rate in Tang's scheme refers to the fraction of correctly detected watermark embedding disks and the detection rate in Wang's scheme refers to the fraction of correctly detected watermark embedding LCR (Local Characteristic Regions). That is, the subimages in our scheme correspond to the disks in Tang's scheme and the LCRs in Wang's scheme, respectively.

Table 2. Comparison of the detection rates (i.e., the fraction of correctly detected watermark embedding regions) under common image processing attacks. (1) Median filter (3×3). (2) Shapening (3×3). (3) Gaussian noise. (4) JPEG 70%. (5) JPEG 50%. (6) JPEG 30%. (7) Median filter (3×3) + JPEG 90%. (8) Sharpening (3×3) + JPEG 90%.

Attacks	Lena			Baboon			Pepper		
	Our Method	Wang's Method	Tang's Method	Our Method	Wang's Method	Tang's Method	Our Method	Wang's Method	Tang's Method
(1)	1.0	0.5	0.125	1.0	0.583	0.182	0.5	0.5	0.25
(2)	1.0	0.5	0.375	1.0	0.5	0.364	1.0	0.625	0.5
(3)	1.0	0.333	0.25	1.0	0.333	0.273	1.0	0.5	0.5
(4)	1.0	0.667	0.625	1.0	0.75	0.728	1.0	0.875	0.75
(5)	1.0	0.667	0.5	1.0	0.75	0.545	0.5	0.75	0.5
(6)	1.0	0.333	0.25	1.0	0.75	0.364	0.5	0.5	0
(7)	1.0	0.5	0.125	1.0	0.583	0.091	0.5	0.5	0.25
(8)	1.0	0.5	0.375	1.0	0.5	0.182	1.0	0.75	0.75

Table 2 clearly shows that our scheme and Wang's scheme successfully pass all the tests while Tang's scheme fails median filtering, JPEG compression 30%, and median filtering with JPEG compression 90%. Our scheme shows better stability than Wang's scheme due to the higher detection ratios under all the attacks. Our method also yields almost equal performance on all three images due to the regulation of the number of strong IFPs on images with different textures whereas Tang's method performs better on high textured images such as Baboon. In summary, the performance of our scheme is much more stable under different attacks in the comparison with Tang's scheme and Wang's scheme. One reason is that our relatively strong IFPs are more stable than those found by the Mexican hat detector and the scale invariant Harris-Laplace detector. These robust IFPs ensure more accurate synchronization between the probe and original watermarked images. Another reason is that the watermark is embedded in the mid-frequencies, which are in positions that are unlikely changed by common image processing attacks.

Table 3 clearly shows that our scheme performs the best in all the desynchronization attacks except the large cropping and local random bending attacks. Specifically, our scheme can successfully resist several attacks Tang's scheme failed to tackle, namely, random relatively large rotations, scaling ratios, and any combination of RST attacks. Our scheme can handle large scaling attacks, which Wang's scheme failed to handle. These successes are mainly due to the following three reasons: 1) Our proposed robust and improved Harris corner detector finds relatively strong IFPs which are more resistant to desynchronization attacks. 2) The strong IFPs-based Delaunay triangle matching and image restoration technique ensures enough matched triangles for accurate self-synchronization under a variety of RST and aspect ratio changing attacks, while the local characteristic region derived from the scale-space theory is not geometrically invariant space, as explained in Wang's scheme. 3) The DFT domain itself is robust to translation and moderate cropping so it can accommodate the cropping attacks and further compensate the slightly inaccurate IFPs-based geometric correction. However, our scheme is more vulnerable to the local random bending attacks than both Tang's and Wang's schemes, due to the possible inaccurate image restoration resulted from the shifts of the bending IFPs or the shifts of the embedding pixels in a limited number (usually less than 9) of the embedding subimages. A large amount of embedding disks in Tang's and Wang's schemes make it more robust to local bending attacks since bending may not affect all the embedding disks and LCRs. Our scheme is also more vulnerable to large cropping attacks since the potential embedding regions may be removed. Tang's and Wang's schemes may survive large cropping attacks as long as a few disks and the LCRs containing the IFPs are not cropped.

Table 3. Comparison of the detection rate (i.e., the fraction of correctly detected watermark embedding regions) under geometric attacks. (1) Removed 8 rows and 16 columns. (2) Cropping 55%. (3) Rotation 5°. (4) Rotation 15°. (5) Rotation 30°. (6) Translation x-10 and y-19. (7) Scaling 0.6. (8) Scaling 0.9. (9) Scaling 1.4. (10) Local random bening. (11) Cropping 10% and JPEG 70%. (12)Rotaion 5° + Scaling 0.9. (13) Translation x-10 and y-10 + Rotation 5° + Scaling 0.9.

Attacks	Lena			Baboon			Pepper		
	Our Method	Wang's Method	Tang's Method	Our Method	Wang's Method	Tang's Method	Our Method	Wang's Method	Tang's Method
(1)	1.0	0.833	0.125	0.780	0.583	0.182	0.375	0.75	0
(2)	0	0.667	0.125	0	0.5	0.182	0	0.625	0
(3)	1.0	0.667	0.375	1.0	0.417	0.273	1.0	0.625	0.25
(4)	1.0	0.5	0.125	1.0	0.333	0.182	0.75	0.5	0
(5)	1.0	0.333	0	1.0	0.333	0	0.75	0.25	0
(6)	1.0	0.833	0.25	1.0	0.833	0.727	1.0	0.625	0.25
(7)	1.0	0.167	0	0.78	0.167	0.091	0.25	0.375	0.25
(8)	1.0	0.5	0.125	1.0	0.417	0.182	0.5	0.375	0.25
(9)	0.5	0.167	0	0.25	0.083	0	0.25	0.25	0
(10)	0	0.5	0.375	0	0.583	0.364	0.25	0.75	0.25
(11)	1.0	0.333	0.25	1.0	0.417	0.182	0.67	0.5	0.25
(12)	1.0	0.5	0	1.0	0.417	0.091	0.5	0.625	0
(13)	0.66	0.333	0	1.0	0.25	0.091	0.5	0.125	0

Table 4. The comparison between the proposed method and Bas's method [15] under different processing and geometric distortion attacks

Attacks	Lena		Airplane		Car	
	Our Method	Bas's Method	Our Method	Bas's Method	Our Method	Bas's Method
No Attack	√	√	√	√	√	√
8×8 Median Filtering	√	×	√	×	√	×
3×3 Gaussian Filtering	√	√	√	√	√	√
Shearing x-1%, y-1%	√	√	√	√	√	√
Shearing x-0%, y-5%	√	√	√	√	√	√
Shearing x-5%, y-5%	√	√	√	√	√	√
Rotation 10°	√	√	√	√	√	√
Scaling 90%	√	√	√	√	√	√
Scaling 80%	√	√	√	√	√	√
JPEG 80%	√	√	√	√	√	√
JPEG 45%	√	√	√	√	√	√
JPEG 30%	√	×	√	×	√	√
Stirmark General Attacks	√	√	√	√	√	√

Table 4 compares the proposed scheme with Bas's scheme [15], which is a feature-based spatial domain method, in terms of the robustness against different attacks such as median filtering, Gaussian filtering, shearing, rotation, scaling, JPEG compression, and Stirmark general attacks. All these tests are performed on images of Lena, Airplane, and Car for a fair comparison. The comparison results upon various common image processing attacks and geometric distortions are listed side by side in Table 4. Since Bas's scheme did not record the detection ratio, we use a " √" to indicate the method successfully detects the watermark after the attack and a " ×" to indicate the method fails to detect the watermark. As shown in Table 4, both methods successfully pass the small shearing, rotation, scaling, and Stirmark general attacks. However, our method has advantages on common image processing tests such as 8×8 median filtering and 30% JPEG compression due to the following reasons: 1) Our method embeds the watermark into the mid-frequencies which are unlikely to be changed by common image processing attacks, while Bas's method introduces an interpolation problem when doing the watermark triangle wrapping in detection. 2) Our method embeds the watermark in the DFT domain, while Bas's scheme is suitable for directly adding watermarks into the spatial domain due to irregular shape of the embedding area. This makes the method vulnerable to image processing distortions.

5.4 Comprehensive Simulation Results under Stirmark Attacks

We performed a variety of attacks on 105 8-bit watermarked grayscale images of size 512×512 using Stirmark 3.1. These images are evenly distributed with high, medium, and low textures according to Eq. (1). That is, the database contains 35 images for each texture level. The overall average PSNR value for these 105 watermarked images is 41.73db. Fig. 6 demonstrates the simulation results of 15 kinds of common attacks on the 105 watermarked images. The simulated attacks are listed on x-axis

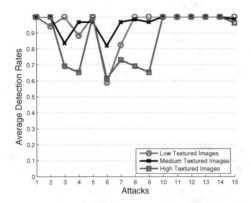

Fig. 6. The average successful detection rates for three kinds of textured images under desynchronization attacks

where all the numerically labeled attacks sequentially correspond to a category of distortions including no attacks, translation, scaling, rotation, cropping up to 5%, linear geometric transform, row and column removal with a maximum of 20 rows and columns removed, median filtering, mean filtering, sharpening, Gaussian filtering, histogram equalization, and JPEG compressions with quality factors of 50%, 40%, and 30%. All the filtering operations use the maximum filter size of 7×7. Each distortion category (i.e., numbers 2 to 12 on x-axis in Fig. 6) contains 3 random attacks. The y-axis summarizes the average detection rates of all images in each texture level under each distortion category. Fig. 6 clearly demonstrates that our scheme achieves good robustness under both image processing and geometric distortions and performs the worst for low and high textured images under the linear geometric attacks. Specifically, the average detection rates for all simulated geometric attacks are 94.89%, 89.75%, and 80.45% for medium, low, and high textured images, respectively. The average detection rates for all simulated image processing attacks are 100%, 100%, and 93.15% for medium, low, and high textured images, respectively. The average detection rates for all simulated attacks are 97.45%, 94.88%, and 86.8% for medium, low, and high textured images, respectively. The overall average detection rate for all images under all simulated attacks is 93.04%.

In summary, the all-around result of our proposed watermark scheme outperforms the peer feature-based schemes. It yields positive detection results for most images with low, medium, and high textures under different desynchronization distortions. It also works well on highly textured images due to the relatively large number of strong IFPs for image restoration. Our proposed scheme achieves a good balance between invisibility and robustness. Specifically, the robust and improved Harris corner detector is capable of finding the relatively strong IFPs for different textured images. The Delaunay triangle matching and image restoration scheme is able to efficiently minimize the synchronization errors and eliminate fake IFPs showed up in the high and extremely high textured images in the matching process. The spread spectrum embedding and detection makes our scheme more resistant to image processing attacks. The perceptually highly textured subimage based embedding scheme helps our system to survive some localized image attacks in Stirmark. However, our scheme does not perform well on extremely low textured images due to its insufficient number of IFPs. It also fails the JPEG compression with a quality factor of lower than 30% due to the missing IFPs resulted from high compression.

6   Conclusions

In this paper, we propose a novel and effective content-based desynchronization resilient watermarking scheme. The major contributions consist of:

- Robust and improved Harris corner detector: This detector is capable of finding the relatively strong IFPs in different textured images. These IFPs are more stable than the feature points extracted by Bas's, Tang's, and Wang's schemes due to the superior performance of the Harris corner detector, the additional noise reduction, the regulation of the density of the IFPs based on the image dimension and texture, and the intersection of IFPs extracted from the pre-attacked images. Consequently, they are more robust against desynchronization attacks.
- Perceptually highly textured subimage based watermark embedding: These embedding subimages carry the same copy of the bipolar watermark bit sequence to improve the robustness of transmitted watermark bits. They also aid the proposed watermark scheme in surviving some localized image attacks in Stirmark.
- Spread-spectrum-based blind watermark embedding and retrieval in the DFT domain: The spread spectrum scheme makes our scheme more resistant to common image processing attacks. The DFT domain ensures more resistant to translation and moderate cropping. The blind retrieval scheme does not require the original image once the probe image is aligned with the original image.
- Delaunay triangle matching and image restoration: This scheme can efficiently eliminate fake IFPs showed up in the highly textured images and accurately determine the possible transformation a probe image may undergo. The determined transformation effectively reduces the synchronization errors without introducing substantial interpolation errors as in Bas's, Tang's, and Wang's schemes, where the affine transform, interpolation, and the image normalization are applied.

The proposed method is robust against a wide variety of tests as indicated in the experimental results. Particularly, it is more robust against JPEG compression and the combination of the geometric distortions with large scaling ratios and rotations than other feature-based watermarking techniques. It works successfully for images with low, medium, and high textures. It can be further improved by developing a more reliable feature extraction method under severe geometric distortions and a more efficient and accurate triangle matching and image restoration method.

The algorithm can be applied to color images by embedding watermark in the luminance component of the color image. In the real world, this watermarking technique can be applied to a lot of different areas, such as photograph, audio, and video.

References

1. Peticolas, F., Anderson, R., Kuhn, M.: Attacks on Copyright Marking Systems. In: Proc. of the 2nd Workshop on Information Hiding, pp. 218–238 (1998)
2. Pereira, S., O'Ruanaidh, J.J.K., Deguillaume, F., Csurka, G., Pun, T.: Template Based Recovery of Fourier-based Watermarks Using Log-Polar and Log-Log Maps. In: Proc. of IEEE Int. Conf. Multimedia Computing Systems, vol. 1, pp. 870–874 (1999)
3. Pereira, S., Pun, T.: Robust Template Matching for Affine Resistant Image Watermarks. IEEE Trans. on Image Processing. 9(6), 1123–1129 (2000)
4. Digimarc Corporation, US patent 5,822,436, Photographic Products and Methods Employing Embedded Information
5. Herrigel, A., Voloshynovskiy, S., Rytsar, Y.B.: Watermark Template Attack. In: Proc. of SPIE Security and Watermarking of Multimedia Contents III, vol. 4314, pp. 394–405 (2001)
6. O'Ruanaidh, J.J.K., Pun, T.: Rotation, Scale, and Translation Invariant Digital Image Watermarking. In: Proc. of IEEE Int. Conf. on Image Processing, pp. 536–539 (1997)
7. O'Ruanaidh, J.J.K., Pun, T.: Rotation, Scale, and Translation Invariant Spread Spectrum Digital Image Watermarking. Signal Processing 66, 303–317 (1998)
8. Zheng, D., Zhao, J., El Saddik, A.: RST-Invariant Digital Image Watermarking Based on Log-Polar Mapping and Phase Correlation. IEEE Trans. on Circuits and Systems for Video Technology. 13(8), 753–765 (2003)
9. Lin, C.Y., Wu, M., Bloom, J.A., Cox, I.J., Miller, M.L., Lui, Y.M.: Rotation, Scale, and Translation Resilient Watermarking for Images. IEEE Trans. on Image Processing. 10(5), 767–782 (2001)
10. Alghoniemy, M., Tewfik, A.H.: Geometric Distortion Correction Through Image Normalization. In: Proc. of IEEE Int. Conf. Multimedia Expo., vol. 3, pp. 1291–1294 (2000)
11. Alghoniemy, M., Tewfik, A.H.: Image Watermarking by Moment Invariants. In: Proc. of IEEE Int. Conf. Image Processing, vol. 2, pp. 73–76 (2000)
12. Alghoniemy, M., Tewfik, A.H.: Geometric Invariance in Image Watermarking. IEEE Trans. on Image Processing. 13(2), 145–153 (2004)
13. Kim, H.S., Lee, H.K.: Invariant Image Watermark Using Zernike Moments. IEEE Trans. on Circuit and Systems for Video Technology. 13(8), 766–775 (2003)
14. Xin, Y., Liao, S., Pawlak, M.: Geometrically Robust Image Watermarking Via Pseudo-Zernike Moments. In: Proc. of Canadian Conf. Electrical and Computer Engineering, vol. 2, pp. 939–942 (2004)
15. Bas, P., Chassery, J.M., Macq, B.: Geometrically Invariant Watermarking Using Feature Points. IEEE Trans. on Image Processing. 11(9), 1014–1028 (2002)
16. Seo, J., Yoo, C.: Localized Image Watermarking Based on Feature Points of Scale-Space Representation. Pattern Recognition 37(7), 1365–1375 (2004)
17. Seo, J., Yoo, C.: Image Watermarking Based on Invariant Regions of Scale-Space Representation. IEEE Trans. on Signal Processing. 54(4), 1537–1549 (2006)
18. Lee, H., Kim, H., Lee, H.: Robust Image Watermarking Using Local Invariant Features. Optical Engineering 45(3), 1–11 (2006)
19. Tang, C.W., Hang, H.M.: A Feature-Based Robust Digital Image Watermarking Scheme. IEEE Trans. on Signal Processing. 51(4), 950–959 (2003)
20. Wang, X., Wu, J., Niu, P.: A New Digital Image Watermarking Algorithm Resilient to Desynchronization Attacks. IEEE Trans. on Information Forensics Security. 2(4), 655–663 (2007)

21. Harris, C., Stephen, M.: A Combined Corner and Edge Detector. In: Proc. of the 4th Alvey Vision Conf., pp. 147–151 (1988)
22. Pickholtz, R.L., Schilling, D.L., Milstein, L.B.: Theory of Spread Spectrum Communications – A Tutorial. IEEE Trans. on Communications. COM 30, 855–884 (1982)
23. Hwang, M.S., Chang, C.C., Hwang, K.F.: A Watermarking Technique Based on One-Way Hashing Functions. IEEE Trans. on Consumer Electronics 25, 286–294 (1999)
24. Hartung, F., Girod, B.: Watermarking of Uncompressed and Compressed Video. Signal Processing 66, 283–301 (1998)
25. Pranata, S., Guan, Y.L., Chua, H.C.: BER Formulation for the Blind Retrieval of MPEG Video Watermark. In: Petitcolas, F.A.P., Kim, H.-J. (eds.) IWDW 2002. LNCS, vol. 2613, pp. 91–104. Springer, Heidelberg (2003)
26. Barni, M., Podilchuk, C.I., Bartolini, F., Delp, E.J.: Watermark Embedding: Hiding a Signal within a Cover Image. IEEE Communications Magazine 39, 102–108 (2001)
27. Bertin, E., Marchand-Maillet, S., Chassery, J.M.: Optimization in Voronoi Diagrams. Kluwer, Dordrecht (1994)
28. Barber, C.B., Dobkin, D.P., Huhdanpaa, H.T.: The Quickhull Algorithm for Convex Hulls. ACM Trans. on Mathematical Software. 22(4), 469–483 (1996)
29. Hsieh, M.S., Tseng, D.C.: Perceptual Digital Watermarking for Image Authentication in Electronic Commerce. Electronic Commerce Research 4, 157–170 (2004)

Robust Watermarking in Slides of Presentations by Blank Space Coloring: A New Approach

Tsung-Yuan Liu[1] and Wen-Hsiang Tsai[1,2]

[1] National Chiao Tung University, Department of Computer Science,
National Chiao Tung University, Hsinchu 300, Taiwan
gis91811@cis.nctu.edu.tw
[2] Asia University, Department of Computer Science and Information Engineering,
Asia University, Taichung, 413, Taiwan
whtsai@cis.nctu.edu.tw

Abstract. A new robust method to embed imperceptibly a watermark image into the slides of a presentation is proposed. The watermark is partitioned into blocks and embedded into the space characters existing in the slides in a repeating pseudo-random sequence. The embedding is achieved by changing the colors of the space characters into new ones which are results of encoding the contents and indices of the blocks. The embedded watermark is resilient against many common modifications on slides, including copying and pasting of slides; insertion, deletion and reordering of slides; slide design changes; and file format conversions. A security key is used during embedding and extraction of a watermark, such that if an offending presentation contains slides taken from presentations watermarked with different security keys, each watermark can be extracted reliably in turn with the respective key using a weighted voting scheme also proposed in this study. Experiments conducted in Microsoft PowerPoint confirm the feasibility of the proposed method. On average, a recognizable watermark of size 64×64 can be extracted from a presentation containing five watermarked slides. The proposed method is useful for various applications of information hiding involving slides, including slide copyright protection, slide authentication, covert communication through slides, etc.

Keywords: information hiding, slide presentation, watermarking, Microsoft PowerPoint, OpenOffice Impress.

1 Introduction

The rapid development of digital technologies in the past decade has made the reproduction and transmission of digital contents simpler and cheaper as ever. However, digital infringement also arises, and anything of value becomes a possible target for illegal duplications and misuses. Digital watermarking researches [1,2,3] offer copyright protection mechanisms to counter offending uses by embedding watermarks into media to prove their ownerships and reveal their distributions. Such watermarks should be imperceptibly hidden in the host media,

Y.Q. Shi (Ed.): Transactions on DHMS IV, LNCS 5510, pp. 49–64, 2009.

and must be resilient against probable modifications by offenders. Watermarking in images, for example, should be robust against scaling, cropping, and format conversion attacks. Lin et al. [4] and O' Ruanaidh and Pun [5] have proposed rotation, scaling and translation resilient watermarking methods for images.

Slide presentation is an increasingly popular way of communication, thanks to cheap projectors and a widespread deployment of them in institutions and businesses. Slide presentations are used for numerous purposes, including lecturing, training, idea presentation, and sales reporting. The slides of a presentation usually are crafted carefully and include texts, images, animations, audios, videos, etc., in order to present valuable contents concisely and lively. It is usually desired to protect the copyright of slides. One way for this purpose is to embed digital watermarks into the slides. To the best knowledge of the authors, digital watermarking of slides has not been investigated before. The traditional means to achieve copyright protection of slides is to place an annoying *visible* logo in the slide background.

One scenario of typical attacking on slides is a person composing a presentation simply by stealing slides out of others' presentations. It is desirable that such malpractice be identifiable automatically. Another different application scenario is where there are confidential internal slides and public marketing slides in a company, and while it is perfectly fine to mix those slides in an internal talk, it is undesirable for the confidential slides to be carelessly shown in external presentations. It will be convenient if there is an automatic means to detect whether a set of slides contain any of the confidential slides.

In this paper, a robust watermarking method for slide copyright protection is proposed, which embeds an *invisible* watermark image imperceptibly into the slides of a presentation. The embedded watermark survives common operations performed on the slides, such as copying and pasting of slides, addition of new slides, removal of slides, reordering of slides, editing of slide contents, and modification to the slide design. The last operation is often applied by a presentation designer to quickly change the style of slides for a desired appearance. The fonts, styles, and colors of texts in the slides, among others, are automatically modified according to a slide design template, as seen in the example shown in Fig. 1.

There are two different ways of setting the colors of texts in presentations. The first, more common approach is to select a color from a color palette, and the selected *index* in the color palette is actually stored. The second approach is to directly set the color of the text usually in the RGB color space, which is a triplet specifying the relative intensities of the red, green, and blue components of the color, usually each in the range of 0 to 255, such as (*red*: 0, *green*: 255, *blue*: 255) for the color yellow. A slide editing software application usually allows any of the two approaches to be used for any text in a slide, and it is possible, for example, to have a whole sentence colored using the color palette approach except the first word which is highlighted using a special RGB color.

For automatic modifications of text colors to work when applying different slide design templates, the first approach of text coloring is used. In more details, different slide design templates have different color palettes, and the colors

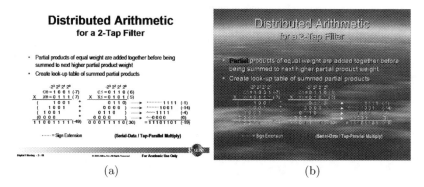

(a)   (b)

Fig. 1. Illustration of slide designs. (a) A slide from a tutorial from Xilinx, Inc. with black texts on white background. (b) The slide in (a) with a slide design template of bluish background applied.

of the titles of a slide, the texts and the hyperlinks in a slide, etc. are set to specific colors from the color palette. The color palette in a design template supplied by a slide editing software application is designed to ensure high contrast texts and an overall appealing appearance. For example, slide templates with a white background will have matching black texts, and templates with a dark background will have texts in light colors. By adhering to the color palettes when editing slides, one can ensure that the colors will be modified appropriately and automatically when selecting a different slide design.

The automatic modifications made during slide design changes pose great challenges to watermarking in slides, and make many previously proposed watermarking techniques ineffective. Text watermarking by making use of the text layout [6] or the LSBs of the text colors, for example, are either removed after the process of applying a slide design, or revealed by the modification. In more details, the method of manipulating the LSBs of the text colors for embedding a watermark does not work because such modifications mean that the colors will no longer be palette entries but specified RGB colors, and thus not altered automatically when a different design template is applied. As an example, the LSB replacement technique has been applied to the word "Partial" in the Fig. 1(a) by changing its color from completely black to dark gray. Although the modification is imperceptible in the original slide, the embedding becomes eye-catching after a slide design modification. The resultant slide after applying a design template that has white text on blue background is shown in Fig. 1(b). The text with the unchanged dark gray color now stands out from the white texts around it. We also note that the visible logo and the copyright information in the slide background have been *removed automatically* after the application of the slide design.

In this paper, we propose to use the *colors of space characters* (called simply as *spaces* hereafter) to embed watermarks, that is, to embed watermark data by altering the color of a space between two words. The colors of the spaces in a slide can be changed without affecting the visual appearance of the slide, and these colors are *unchanged* during application of other slide designs, changing of slide layouts, reordering of slides, reordering of texts in slides, and conversion of file formats, as found in this study. As the spaces are *transparent*, we can manipulate the colors freely for the purpose of information embedding, using either the color palette or the RGB coloring approach, without any visual side-effects. The latter is chosen due to its greater embedding capacity. Specifically, we divide a watermark image into blocks and encode the index and data of each block into a RGB color value which is then taken to replace the original color of a space, accomplishing the embedding of a watermark block's information into a space character. For security, the watermark blocks are embedded into the slides in a random sequence created by a pseudo-number generator with a user-specified key. To extract the embedded watermark, a weighted voting scheme is designed to handle the problem of watermark recovery from presentations that contain watermarked slides and non-watermarked slides. The average number of watermarked slides required to achieve a specified percentage of coverage of an extracted watermark image is also analyzed. Experimental results showing feasibility of the proposed approach is also included.

In the remainder of this paper, the details of the watermark embedding and extraction processes follow in Section 2. Section 3 presents some of our experimental results, and in Section 4 we conclude with some suggestions for future works.

2   Robust Watermarking in Slides of Presentations

In the proposed method, the spaces among the texts in the slides of a presentation are used to embed a watermark, which is assumed to be an $N \times N$ black-and-white image, such as a logo of a company. The image is divided into M blocks, each containing L pixels, where $L = N^2/M$. The L pixel values of each block are concatenated in a raster scan order into a string, which we call a *block data string* in the sequel. The basic idea of watermarking in the proposed approach is to *encode* the data string and the index of each block into an RGB color, with which the color of a text space in a slide is replaced. That is, watermarking here consists of the two steps of *watermark block encoding* and *space color replacement*.

Since a copyright violator might copy only some of the watermarked slides of a presentation, we choose to embed the watermark *repeatedly* throughout the slides. The embedding of the block index along with the block data string means that the embedded data are *invariant* against insertion and reordering of slides or slide contents.

2.1   Watermark Embedding

More specifically, during watermark embedding, the spaces are taken for data embedding *in the reading/presentation order*, that is, the spaces in the first slide are used first in a top-to-bottom and left-to-right order, followed by the spaces in the second slide, and so on. While the blocks of the watermark are embedded into this normal sequence of spaces, the indices of the embedded blocks instead follow a pseudo-random sequence controlled by a key to increase security of data protection. The algorithm below describes the proposed process of watermark embedding.

Algorithm 1: Embedding a watermark image into slides of a presentation.

Input: A set P of slides of a presentation; a watermark image I to be embedded, which is partitioned into M block data strings $B_1, B_2, \ldots, B_M$; and a user-specified key K.

Output: Watermarked slides of P with I embedded by coloring the spaces in P appropriately.

Steps:

1. Generate a random integer sequence $E = i_1, i_2, \ldots, i_M$ in the range of $1, 2, \ldots, M$ without repetitive values, using K and a pseudo-random number generator f.
2. Find all spaces $s_1, s_2, \ldots, s_Q$ in P in the reading/presentation order, and repeat the sequence E for $\lceil Q/M \rceil$ times to arrive at another sequence $E' = j_1, j_2, \ldots, j_R$, where $R = M \times \lceil Q/M \rceil \geq Q$.
3. For each space s_k in P, $1 \leq k \leq Q$, pick out the index j_k in E' and the corresponding block data string B_{j_k}, and encode the pair (j_k, B_{j_k}) into a color C to replace that of s_k in the following way:
   (a) combine j_k and B_{j_k} into an integer $A = j_k \times 2^L + B_{j_k}$, regarding B_{j_k} as an L-bit number;
   (b) compute color $C = (R, G, B)$ by taking the three components respectively to be $B = A \bmod 2^l$, $G = \lfloor A/2^l \rfloor \bmod 2^l$, and $R = \lfloor A/2^{2l} \rfloor$, where each component is assumed to have l bits;
   (c) replace the color of space s_k with C.

The embedding of the blocks of a watermark image in a predefined random sequence as described in the above algorithm has several benefits, as described in the following.

1. A recognizable partial watermark can be extracted if an offender copies only a portion of the watermarked material. Fig. 2 shows two series of watermark images with different percentages of blocks successfully reconstructed. The watermark can be recognized already when only half of the blocks (i.e., $M/2$ blocks) are present.
2. If an offender puts some of the watermarked slides together with other non-watermarked ones, the watermarked slides can still be correctly identified using a weighted voting scheme proposed in this study (described later), which gives more weights to extracted block data strings with indices in right orders defined by the random sequence.
3. Furthermore, if an offender copies watermarked slides from multiple sources with different user keys and watermark images, the individual watermark images can be extracted correctly in turn by using the respective user keys, as confirmed in the experiment.

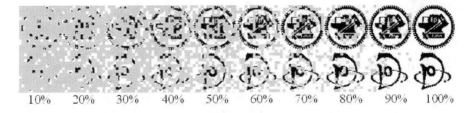

10%   20%   30%   40%   50%   60%   70%   80%   90%   100%

Fig. 2. Two series of watermark logos with different block coverages

2.2   Weighted Voting of Partial Sequences for Watermark Extraction

During watermark extraction, it might happen that a given set of slides includes both watermarked slides and non-watermarked ones, as mentioned previously. Since a space with no embedded data in a non-watermarked slide also has a color value which may be as well decoded into a block data string and a block index, a weighted voting scheme is proposed in this study to identify the spaces that really contain watermark data, so that a correct watermark can be reconstructed. We assume that the block indices extracted from non-watermarked slides to be uniformly distributed in the range of $\{1, 2, \ldots, M\}$.

More specifically, since an offender usually copies a complete slide or an entire sentence in a slide at a time, the order of the spaces in the copied contents are preserved. The basic idea of the proposed weighted voting technique is to analyze the sequence of block indices extracted from the spaces of the slides of a suspect presentation, and check whether the extracted sequence follows an expected sequence. Blocks that follow the expected sequence are more likely to contain watermark data than those that do not, and thus are given larger weights in using them for reconstructing the watermark image.

We denote the sequence of pairs of block indices and block data strings that have been extracted from the spaces of a suspect presentation as $S = \{(j_1, B_1), (j_2, B_2), \ldots, (j_Q, B_Q)\}$, where j_k is the index of block data string B_k. The expected sequence $E = \{i_1, i_2, \ldots, i_M\}$, as generated by Algorithm 1, is a random integer sequence in the range of $\{1, 2, \ldots, M\}$ without repetitive values. As the blocks of the watermark are embedded repeatedly according to the sequence E, we regard the sequence to be cyclic and use the new notation E^+ to specify a sequence of arbitrary length formed by concatenating sequence E repeatedly. Also, we use the notation $\{j_k, j_{k+1}, \ldots, j_l\} \subset E^+$ to mean that the sequence $\{j_k, j_{k+1}, \ldots, j_l\}$ is a subsequence of E^+.

Now consider a text space s_k which does not contain previously embedded watermark data, and from which the pair (j_k, B_k) in S is extracted. There are three cases here.

1. For $k = 1$ (corresponding to the case that s_k is the first space of the suspect presentation), the probability that the index sequence $\{j_k, j_{k+1}\} \subset E^+$ is $1/2^M$, irrespective of whether the block with index j_{k+1} contains embedded watermark data or not. The probability that $\{j_k, j_{k+1}\} \not\subset E^+$ is $1 - 1/2^M$.

2. For $k = Q$ (corresponding to the case that s_k is the last space of the suspect presentation), the probability that $\{j_{k-1}, j_k\} \subset E^+$ is $1/2^M$, irrespective of whether the block with index j_{k-1} contains embedded watermark data or not. The probability that $\{j_{k-1}, j_k\} \not\subset E^+$ is $1 - 1/2^M$.

3. For $1 < k < Q$, the probability that $\{j_{k-1}, j_k, j_{k+1}\} \subset E^+$ is $1/2^M \times 1/2^M = 1/2^{2M}$, irrespective of whether the blocks with block indices j_{k-1} and j_{k+1} contain embedded watermark data or not. The probability that $\{j_{k-1}, j_k, j_{k+1}\} \not\subset E^+$ but $\{j_{k-1}, j_k\} \subset E^+$ is $1/2^M \times (1 - 1/2^M)$, and so is the probability that $\{j_{k-1}, j_k, j_{k+1}\} \not\subset E^+$ but $\{j_k, j_{k+1}\} \subset E^+$. The probability that $\{j_{k-1}, j_k\} \not\subset E^+$ and $\{j_k, j_{k+1}\} \not\subset E^+$ is $(1 - 1/2^M) \times (1 - 1/2^M)$.

We propose to weigh the block data strings in S according to the minus base-2 logarithm values of the above probabilities in using the data string values in the process of watermark extraction. That is, for $k = 1$, block data string B_k is given a weight of $-\log_2(1/2^M)$, which we denote as W_A, if $\{j_k, j_{k+1}\} \subset E^+$; and if $\{j_k, j_{k+1}\} \not\subset E^+$, then block data string B_k is given a weight of $-\log_2(1 - 1/2^M)$, which we denote as W_B. Similarly, if $k = Q$, block data string B_k receives a weight of W_A if $\{j_{k-1}, j_k\} \subset E^+$, and a weight of W_B if $\{j_{k-1}, j_k\} \not\subset E^+$. For $1 < k < Q$, the block data string B_k is given a weight of $-\log_2(1/2^{2M}) = 2W_A$ if $\{j_{k-1}, j_k, j_{k+1}\} \subset E^+$, a weight of $-\log_2[1/2^M \times (1 - 1/2^M)] = W_A + W_B$ if either $\{j_{k-1}, j_k\} \subset E^+$ or $\{j_k, j_{k+1}\} \subset E^+$, and a weight of $-log2[(1 - 1/2^M) \times (1 - 1/2^M)] = 2W_B$ if none of the above are true. The block data strings with the largest weights are then chosen for watermark reconstruction, as described in the following algorithm.

Algorithm 2: Weighted voting of partial index sequences for watermark extraction.

Input: An expected sequence $E = \{i_1, i_2, \ldots, i_M\}$; an input sequence of extracted block indices and data strings $S = \{(j_1, B'_1), (j_2, B'_2), \ldots, (j_Q, B'_Q)\}$; and a threshold T.

Output: Block data strings $B_1, B_2, \ldots, B_M$ of the M blocks that comprise a watermark image I.

Steps:

1. Initialize $W_1, W_2, \ldots, W_M$ to be M empty sequences of 2-tuples.
2. For each pair (j_k, B'_k) in S with block index j_k and block data string B'_k, $1 \leq k \leq Q$, add the pair (B'_k, W) to the sequence W_{j_k} where:
   (a) for $k = 1$, $W = W_A$ if $\{j_k, j_{k+1}\} \subset E^+$, and $W = W_B$ if $\{j_k, j_{k+1}\} \not\subset E^+$;
   (b) for $k = Q$, $W = W_A$ if $\{j_{k-1}, j_k\} \subset E^+$, and $W = W_B$ if $\{j_{k-1}, j_k\} \not\subset E^+$;
   (c) for $1 < k < Q$, $W = 2W_A$ if $\{j_{k-1}, j_k, j_{k+1}\} \subset E^+$; else $W = W_A + W_B$ if either $\{j_{k-1}, j_k\} \subset E^+$ or $\{j_k, j_{k+1}\} \subset E^+$; or else $W = 2W_B$.
3. Derive the data string B_l of the lth block of I as follows where $1 \leq l \leq M$:
   (a) sum up the weights with identical data strings in W_l;
   (b) select the data string $B'_{\max}$ in W_l with the maximum weight $W_{\max}$;
   (c) if there are no such $B'_{\max}$'s, or if there were multiple such $B'_{\max}$'s, or if $W_{\max}$ is smaller than the threshold T, then regard B_l as missing, and

represent the lth block as a gray-colored block; else set the data string B_l to be $B'_{\max}$.

As an example, let $M = 4$, $E = \{3, 1, 4, 2\}$, $S = \{(2, A), (3, B), (1, C), (4, D), (1, E), (4, F), (2, A)\}$, and $T = 0$. Then $E^+ = \{3, 1, 4, 2, 3, 1, 4, 2, 3, \ldots\}$. After Step 2 of the above algorithm, we have $W_1 = \{(C, 2W_A), (E, W_A + W_B)\}$ because the partial data set $\{(3, B), (1, C), (4, D)\}$ in S forms an index sequence of $\{3, 1, 4\}$ which fits well with the first three indices of E^+, yielding the result of the pair $(C, 2W_A)$ in W_1; and the partial data set $\{(1, E), (4, F)\}$ forms an index sequence of $\{1, 4\}$ found also in E^+, yielding $(E, W_A + W_B)$ in W_1. In similar ways, we can compute $W_2 = \{(A, W_A), (A, W_A)\}$, $W_3 = \{(B, 2W_A)\}$, and $W_4 = \{(D, W_A + W_B), (F, W_A)\}$. Accordingly, in Step 3 the block data strings P_1, P_2, P_3 and P_4 are set to C, A, B and D, respectively, with the weighting for data string A summed to be $2W_A$.

The above method ensures that sequences of blocks that contain watermark data dominate during the watermark image reconstruction in Step 3. However, if only a small portion of the watermarked contents are copied, then some of the blocks of the reconstructed watermark image may be missing. The threshold T is useful in this case, where setting T to a large value causes noise from non-watermarked blocks to be ignored. A value of at least W_A is recommended, since block weights from any partial sequences of the watermark contents are at least of the value of W_A.

In Step 3c of the algorithm, instead of ignoring all of the multiple candidate block data strings with the same weights, we could use a voting algorithm to restore the correct watermark pixel values amid noise, as described in the following.

Algorithm 3: Intra-block voting for pixel value reconstruction.

Input: A set S_C of V block data strings $B_1, B_2, \ldots, B_V$; and an adjustable threshold H, where $0.5 \leq H < 1$.

Output: Colors (black or white) $p_1, p_2, \ldots, p_L$ of the pixels comprising a block P of a watermark image.

Steps:

1. Set the color of each pixel p_j, $1 \leq j \leq L$, as follows:
   (a) count the number of blocks in S_C, whose corresponding pixel value is *black* (i.e., with bit value 1), and denote the number as C_B;
   (b) count the number of blocks in S_C, whose corresponding pixel value is *white* (i.e., with bit value 0), and denote the number as C_W;
   (c) set the color of p_j to be black if $C_B/V > H$; else set the color of the pixel to be white if $C_W/V > H$; or else set the color of the pixel to be gray, meaning the pixel color was indeterminate.

The basic idea of the above algorithm is that the block data strings decoded from text spaces that do not contain watermark data can be considered to contain random values. For each pixel, the number of blocks that have the corresponding pixel value of black is approximately the same as that having a pixel value of white. The assumption of inclusion of the correct block data string causes the scale to tip towards the correct side. To handle the case where no correct blocks is available, as the case may be when only a few watermarked slides are taken, the value of H can be increased to reduce the resulting noise in the extracted watermark image.

2.3   Watermark Extraction

In the proposed watermark extraction process, the spaces in the slides of a suspect presentation are analyzed to extract a sequence of block indices and block data strings. Algorithm 2 is then used to analyze the extracted block indices and data strings to reconstruct the previously embedded watermark image. The algorithm below describes the details.

Algorithm 4: Extracting a watermark image from the slides of a suspect presentation.

Input: A set P of slides of a suspect presentation and a key K.

Output: A watermark image in P comprised by M block data strings B_1, $B_2, \ldots, B_M$.

Steps:

1. Generate the random integer sequence $E = \{i_1, i_2, \ldots, i_M\}$ in the range of $\{1, 2, \ldots, M\}$ without repetitive values, using K and the same pseudo-random number generator f used during watermark embedding.
2. Initialize S to be an empty sequence of pairs of block indices and block data strings.
3. Find all spaces $s_1, s_2, \ldots, s_Q$ in P in the same order as that of embedding, and for each space s_k, $1 \leq k \leq Q$, decode the color $C = (R, G, B)$ of s_k into a pair (j, D) of a block index j and a block data string D and put it into S in the following way:
   (a) compute an integer $A = R \times 2^{2l} + G \times 2^l + B$, assuming that the RGB color space has l bits per channel;
   (b) compute j and D as $j = \lfloor A/2^L \rfloor$ and $D = A \bmod 2^L$, respectively (because presumably $A = D \times 2^L + j$ according to Step 3a of Algorithm 1);
   (c) add (j, D) to S.
4. Reconstruct $B_1, B_2, \ldots, B_M$ using Algorithm 2 with E and S as inputs.

2.4   Embedding Capacity and Expected Reconstruction Coverage

When embedding the blocks of a watermark image into the spaces of slides, popular slide presentation formats like Microsoft PowerPoint and OpenOffice Impress can be used. Eight bits per color channel and hence 24 bits can be embedded into each text space in slides of such formats. This embedding capacity allows us to embed a black-and-white watermark image as large as 64×64 into the slides of a presentation of normal sizes. When embedding a watermark image of such a size, we first divide it into $M = 256$ blocks with each block containing $L = 16$ pixels. Each space then is used to store an 8-bit block index and 16-bits of pixel values. For a presentation we use in this study that contains slides with 40 spaces per slide on average, only seven slides is required to embed a complete watermark, and four slides may be sufficient to extract a recognizable watermark. The watermark image is embedded repeatedly into the slides as mentioned previously. Fig. 2 shows a series of 64×64 logos with different coverages that have been divided into 256 blocks of 4×4 pixels. If a smaller watermark image was used during watermark embedding, the number of spaces required to extract a recognizable watermark is reduced.

When an offender takes slides selectively, instead of consecutively, from a watermarked presentation, the block data contained in these slides may overlap with each other, meaning that a higher number of spaces are required to reconstruct a recognizable watermark. We estimate the number of watermarked spaces required to achieve the desired watermark image coverage by assuming that the offender draws R spaces from a watermarked presentation randomly, and that the block index in each of the drawn spaces is uniformly distributed in the sample space $\{1, 2, \ldots, M\}$. We denote the R random block indices as $i_1, i_2, \ldots, i_R$, and G the number of *distinct values* in $\{i_1, i_2, \ldots, i_R\}$ over the value M. In other words, G is the percentage of the blocks of the watermark that is contained in the R randomly chosen spaces, and the *expected coverage* $E(G)$ is the expected percentage of the watermark image that can be reconstructed. To derive $E(G)$, we first introduce random variables $I_1, I_2, \ldots, I_M$, where $I_j = 1$ if none of the values of $i_1, i_2, \ldots, i_R$ is equal to j, and $I_j = 0$ if at least one of the values is equal to j. The probability that $I_j = 1$ is $(1 - 1/M)^R$, and the expected value of I_j is thus $E(I_j) = (1 - 1/M)^R$. Since $G = [\sum(1 - I_j)]/M$, the expected coverage is

$$E(G) = E\left(\frac{\sum(1 - I_j)}{M}\right)$$
$$= \frac{M - \sum E(I_j)}{M}$$
$$= 1 - (1 - 1/M)^R. \tag{1}$$

From (1), the number of spaces R required to result in a desired expected coverage $E(G)$ is

$$R = \frac{\log(1 - E(G))}{\log(1 - 1/M)}. \tag{2}$$

Using the above equation, we can estimate the number of spaces that are required to achieve a recognizable watermark image. A recognizable watermark should have at least 50% coverage, as seen in Fig. 2 and Fig. 3. With $E(G) = 0.5$ and $M = 256$, approximately $R = 178$ spaces, or about 5 slides, for a presentation containing on average 40 spaces per slide, are required according to Equation (2); and for a good quality watermark image with 80% coverage, approximately 412 spaces, or 11 slides, are required. In practice, images and drawings in slides should also be utilized during watermark embedding by using information hiding techniques for these media [1,7,8] to reduce the amount of slides required for a desired reconstructed watermark.

Fig. 3. Illustration of watermark reconstruction coverage. (a) Three watermarks each with coverage of 50%; (b) the three watermarks with 80% coverage.

2.5   Robustness of Proposed Method against Common Operations

The watermark embedded into the slides of a presentation using the proposed method is resilient against many common operations performed on slides. In particular, the embedded watermark is robust against changes to the slide design template, as described in the introduction, whereas traditional visible logos are removed automatically in the process. Also, the automatic changes to the text and background colors lure a thieve to believe that no color information could have survived the transformation.

The watermark is also robust against copying and pasting of watermarked slides, as the colors and orderings of the spaces in the slides are unaltered during these types of processes. If we assume reasonably that there are at least two spaces in a slide, the block data strings embedded in the spaces of the slide will receive a sufficiently large weight using the proposed scheme for correct reconstruction of the embedded watermark image. Reordering of the slides in a presentation is a similar operation to copying and pasting of slides, and has little impact on correct watermark extraction. Reordering of slide contents is often conducted by moving pictures and text blocks around or by exchanging the order of the sentences in a slide. The former operation does not have any effect, while the latter is the same as reordering of slides if there are at least two spaces in a sentence.

Insertion of new non-watermarked slides or watermarked slides created with a different key into a slide set does not affect the watermarked contents, but only increases the amount of noise during reconstruction. Algorithms 2 and 3 are capable of selecting out the correct watermark data amid noise, as is verified in the experiments conducted in this study, where correct watermark images were reconstructed from watermarked slides that have been reordered and put together with slides that have been watermarked with different keys.

The proposed method is also resilient against removals of slides or slide contents, as long as sufficient watermarked contents remain. Experiments have shown that a recognizable watermark of size 64×64 can be reconstructed from approximately five watermarked slides.

Lastly, the watermark embedded using the proposed method has been proven to be robust against file format conversion attacks. Specifically, a presentation with slides watermarked using the proposed method was first saved in Microsoft PowerPoint in its PPT format. The file was then opened by another presentation software, OpenOffice Impress, and saved in the OpenDocument ODP format.

The ODP format file was then reopened by Impress, and finally saved back into the PPT format by Impress. Fig. 4(a) shows the first two slides of a test presentation before file format conversion, and Fig. 4(b) shows the same two slides after the above described format conversions from PPT to ODP and back to PPT. We note that the font type (changed from *Arial* to *Times New Roman*) and the font size (changed from 42pt to 44pt) of the title on the first slide, and the drawing on the second slide, among others, were changed during the file format conversions. The embedded watermark image, however, was untouched during the process and can be perfectly reconstructed.

3   Experimental Results

We implemented the proposed watermark embedding and extraction methods in C#.NET, and conducted a series of experiments using the popular presentation editing application Microsoft PowerPoint 2003. We use the *Automation* technique provided by Microsoft [9] to process PowerPoint presentation files. We have collected slides from the presentations of some projects we are currently investigating, as well as some presentations that are available from the web [10,11,12]. The average number of spaces per slide in these samples ranges from 35 to 60. Three slides with the characteristics listed in Table 1 are chosen for the experiments.

In the experiments, three logo images, each of size 64×64, are used as watermarks. Each of them was divided into 256 blocks of 4×4 pixels each, and individually embedded into the slides of the three presentations with different security keys using Algorithm 1. A presentation was then constructed by drawing slides randomly from the watermarked presentations. Specifically, N slides were drew randomly from each of the three presentations and then combined to form an experimental presentation that contains $3N$ slides. The three watermark logos were then extracted from the experimental presentation with the three respective keys in turn using Algorithm 4. The number of pixels that were correctly reconstructed in each of the three extracted watermark logos was counted, and the fractions of correct pixel extraction for the three images were recorded for each trial. This process was repeated 10,000 times for each value of N ranging from 1 to 19, and the average correct coverages of the three extracted watermarks are plotted in Fig. 5. To reconstruct a recognizable extracted watermark with

Table 1. Characteristics of presentations used in the experiments

	A	B	C
Number of slides	35	28	51
Total number of spaces	2086	1029	2605
Average number of spaces per slide	59.6	36.8	51.1
Maximum number of spaces in a slide	352	159	339
Minimum number of spaces in a slide	0	1	1
Standard deviation of spaces per slide	73.0	37.4	53.7

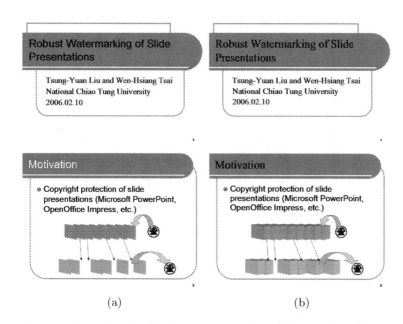

(a)   (b)

Fig. 4. An experimental result of file format conversion. (a) Two slides in Microsoft PowerPoint. (b) The two slides after file format conversion from PPT to ODP and back.

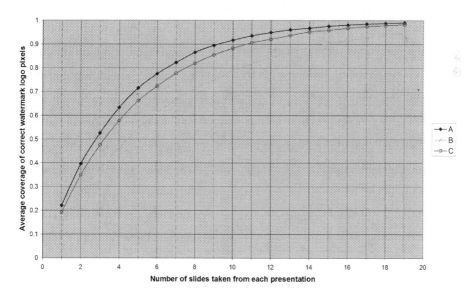

Fig. 5. Plot of average correct watermark pixel extractions from presentations constructed from randomly drawn slides

N = 3   N = 10

Fig. 6. An experimental result of the three extracted watermarks with N ranging from 3 to 10

at least 50% correct coverage, 3, 5, and 4 slides are required from presentations A, B, and C, respectively; and to reconstruct one with 80% correct coverage, 7, 11, and 8 slides are required from A, B, and C, respectively.

Fig. 6 shows one result of the three extracted watermarks for N ranging from 3 to 10. The result is imperfect because of the large variations in the number of spaces in each slide. Specifically, some slides in the presentations used in the experiments contain more than one hundred spaces. The selection of just a few of these slides will result in perfect reconstruction of the watermark image. For example, the presence of a slide from presentation C that contains 339 spaces (shown in Fig. 1) alone in an offending presentation allows the perfect reconstruction of the embedded watermark. On the contrary, if slides that contain less than ten spaces were picked during a trial of the experiment, then many blocks of the reconstructed watermark image will be missing. We note that the randomly constructed presentation contains slides watermarked with a key different to the one used for extraction, and can thus include incorrect data for these missing blocks. However, since such erroneous blocks do not follow the expected sequence specific for the extraction key, they are effectively filtered out by the proposed weighted voting scheme, as observed in the figure. The average percentages of the watermark that was incorrectly recovered fall in the range of 0.02% ∼ 0.24% in the experiments.

The plot in Fig. 5 was normalized by multiplying the number of slides taken from each of the presentation by the average number of spaces per slide. The normalized plot, with the average number of spaces taken from each presentation as the x-axis, is shown in Fig. 7. It is clear that the performance of the proposed method is relatively insensitive to the properties of the slides in a presentation. The estimated coverage of the extracted watermark derived as Equation (1) is also plotted in the figure for comparison.

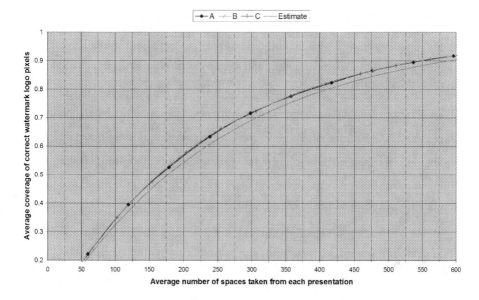

Fig. 7. Normalized plot of average correct watermark pixel extractions from presentations constructed from randomly drawn slides

To achieve a correct coverage of 50% and 80% respectively, approximately 165 and 385 spaces are required respectively according to the figure, which are close to the theoretical estimates of 178 and 412. The actual experimental results are slightly better than the theoretical estimates because we assumed that all spaces were drawn randomly for the estimate, whereas in the experiments a whole slide that contains spaces in sequence was taken at a time. As observed in the experimental results, the interferences between the different sets of watermarked slides have been eliminated by the application of the proposed weighted voting scheme.

4   Conclusions and Future Works

In this paper we described a novel method for embedding watermark images into the slides of presentations. The watermarked presentation is visually indistinguishable from the original version, and is robust against most common editing operations. Specifically, the watermarked presentation is resilient against insertions, removals, and reordering of slides, copying and pasting of slides, changes to the slide design templates, and file format conversions. Furthermore, if slides taken from multiple presentations that have been watermarked using different keys are combined into a single presentation, each of the previously embedded watermark images can be individually extracted correctly with the respective keys using the proposed method. For example, a lecturer may assemble a presentation by taking slides from presentations supplied by a book publisher and presentations taken from online course pages. If watermarks have been embedded in the slides of the source presentations, we can extract the watermarks from the assembled slide presentation using the proposed method.

The watermark embedding and extraction methods have been tested using the popular presentation software Microsoft PowerPoint, and good experimental results demonstrate the feasibility and resilience of the proposed method. On average, five slides taken from a watermarked presentation using a certain security key is sufficient to extract a recognizable watermark of size 64×64.

Due to the robustness of the proposed method, adaptability of the proposed method for the applications of covert communication, slide authentication, or text annotation is certainly plausible, and can be pursued in future works. Other data hiding techniques appropriate for slides of presentations and other popular file formats are also good future research topics.

References

1. Petitcolas, F.A.P., Anderson, R.J., Kuhn, M.G.: Information hiding – a survey. Proceedings of IEEE 87(7), 1062–1078 (1999)
2. Johnson, N.F., Duric, Z., Jajodia, S.: Information hiding: steganography and watermarking: attacks and countermeasures. Advances in information security, vol. 1, p. 137. Kluwer Academic Publishers, Dordrecht (2001)
3. Cox, I.J., Miller, M.L.: The first 50 years of electronic watermarking. EURASIP Journal on Applied Signal Processing 2002(2), 126–132 (2002)
4. Lin, C.Y., Wu, M., Bloom, J.A., Cox, I.J., Miller, M.L., Lui, Y.M.: Rotation, scale, and translation resilient watermarking for images. IEEE Trans. Image Processing 10(5), 767–782 (2001)
5. Ó Ruanaidh, J.J.K., Pun, T.: Rotation, translation and scale invariant digital image watermarking. In: IEEE Signal Processing Society 1997 International Conference on Image Processing (ICIP 1997), Santa Barbara, California (1997)
6. Brassil, J.T., Low, S., Maxemchuk, N.F.: Copyright protection for the electronic distribution of text documents. Proceedings of IEEE 87(7), 1181–1196 (1999)
7. Wu, D.C., Tsai, W.H.: A steganographic method for images by pixel-value differencing. Pattern Recognition Letters 24(9-10), 1613–1626 (2003)
8. Solachidis, V., Pitas, I.: Watermarking polygonal lines using fourier descriptors. IEEE Computer Graphics and Applications 24(3), 44–51 (2004)
9. Microsoft: Microsoft Office 1997 Visual Basic: programmer's guide. Microsoft, Redmond (1997)
10. Muterspaugh, M., Liu, H., Gao, W.: Thomson proposal outline for WRAN, proposal for IEEE P802.22 Wireless RANs, doc.: IEEE802.22-05/0096r1 (November 2005)
11. Tseng, S.S., Tsai, W.H.: High confidence information systems mid-term report, NSC advanced technologies and applications for next generation information networks (October 2002)
12. Xilinx: Digital filtering, DSP design flow (2003),
    http://users.ece.gatech.edu/~hamblen/4006/xup/dsp_flow/slides/

A Novel Least Distortion Linear Gain Model for Halftone Image Watermarking Incorporating Perceptual Quality Metrics

Weina Jiang, Anthony T.S. Ho, and Helen Treharne

The Department of Computing
University of Surrey
Guildford, GU2 7XH, UK
{W.Jiang}@Surrey.ac.uk

Abstract. In this paper, a least distortion approach is proposed for halftone image watermarking. The impacts of distortion and tonality problems in halftoning are analyzed. An iterative linear gain model is developed to optimize perceptual quality of watermarking halftone images with efficient computation complexity $O(1)$. An optimum linear gain for data hiding error diffusion is derived and mapped into a standard linear gain model, with the tonality evaluated using the average power spectral density. As compared with Fu and Au's data hiding error diffusion method, our experiments show that our proposed linear gain model can achieve an improvement of between 6.5% to 12% using weighted signal-to-noise ratio (WSNR) and an improvement of between 11% to 23% measured by visual image fidelity (VIF).

1 Introduction

Halftoning is an important operation that transforms conventional grayscale and color images into bi-level images that are particularly useful for print-and-scan processes [1]. In fact many images and documents displayed in newsprint and facsimile are halftone images. The problems of copyrights protection and unauthorized tampering of digital content, particularly in printed and scanned form, are becoming increasingly widespread that need to be addressed. As such, digital watermarking [2] can be very useful in protecting printable halftone images for business, legal and law enforcement applications. In the recent literature, researchers have proposed a variety of approaches to data hiding and watermarking but many were designed for multi-tone images and could not be applied for halftone image directly.

In general, halftone watermarking approaches are classified as (1) error diffusion-based halftone watermarking. a watermark is embedded into a halftone image during an error diffusion process. In [3], Fu and Au proposed this approach. The main idea is that performing self-toggling in N pseudo random locations, the error of self-toggling plus the error of standard error diffusion halftoning diffuse to neighboring pixels. A private key is required in the verifier

Y.Q. Shi (Ed.): Transactions on DHMS IV, LNCS 5510, pp. 65–83, 2009.

side to generate N pseudo random locations to be used for retrieving the watermark. In [4], Sherry and Savakis proposed data hiding cell parity (DHCP) and data hiding mask toggling (DHMT) based on Fu and Au's approach to improve the halftone perceptual quality. However, the image quality was affected due to the frequency distortion arises by error diffusion process itself. In this paper, the quality preserving solution has been studied to compensate the distortion issue while watermarking embedding; (2) data hiding in multi-halftone images in order to increase capacity. A watermark was embedded into two or more halftoning images, revealing the watermark when these embedded images were overlaid [5]. In [6], the watermark was decoded using a look up table (LUT). The above methods have the disadvantage that the extracted watermark contains residual patterns from the two overlaid images, thus reduces the fidelity of the extracted watermark image. In [5], an iterative isotropic algorithm and coordinate projection were proposed to solve the problem described above. However, the contrast of the embedded images was found to be lower than using other methods. (3) watermarking in dither halftoning. Watermarking in dither halftone images is proposed in [7][8]. The advantage of dither halftone watermarking is low complexity but the image quality will be degraded. Besides, the embedded capacity is non-flexible. In [9], high quality progressive coding was proposed to embed a watermark into a dithered halftone image but the quality was found to be lower than Fu and Au's method [3]. (4) watermarking in Direct Binary Search (DBS) halftoning. In [10], Kacker and Allebach proposed a framework to address the feasibility of a joint halftoning and watermarking scheme for a grayscale image. The block-based spread spectrum watermarking scheme was applied to a grayscale image, along with a DBS halftoning algorithm. A HVS-based error metric was used to analyze the watermarked halftone image. This joint method was found to provide better quality based on the watermark correlation criterion. However, the computational requirements increased for some applications, which could be a potential drawback.

Halftone quality and robustness are the two main challenges for watermarking halftone images. The robustness of watermarking can be enhanced by incorporating error correction coding [11]. However, data hiding error diffusion is not trivial since embedding data into halftone image downgrades the perceptual quality of halftone image. It is difficult to increase robustness without causing a significant amount of perceptual distortion because error correction coding requires high capacity of watermarks to be embedded into halftone image.

In this paper, we analyze the sharpening distortion in data hiding error diffusion and propose a watermarking linear gain model to address how to compensate perceptual quality via minimizing distortion in data hiding error diffusion of halftone images. In error diffusion halftoning, a grayscale image is quantized into one bit pixel via an *error diffusion kernel* [1][12]. As a consequence, it sharpens the image and adds quantization noise resulting in artifacts and idle tones. However, some artifacts and idle tones are incurred even without watermark embedding. The main aim of our proposed method is to preserve the least distortion data hiding error diffusion in halftone images.

Furthermore, we propose the use of average power spectrum $\overline{PSD}$ to measure harmonic distortion of halftone and embedded halftone images, analogous to total harmonic distortion (THD) [13]. Experiments show that the proposed iterative halftone watermarking model not only optimizes the perceptual quality of watermarking halftone images but also reduces tonality, with overall perceptual quality significantly better than Fu and Au's method tested on similar images.

The rest of the paper is organized as follows. In Section 2, related work is reviewed. In Section 3, we describe a watermarking embedding process and how the distortion can be modeled and eliminated via an iterative linear gain model. In Section 4, an iterative linear gain halftoning embedding is designed and implemented. In Section 5, we perform experiments to compare perceptual image quality of our proposed method to that of Fu and Au's approach. also the tonality problem is analyzed. We conclude and discuss future work in Section 6.

2   Related Work

Halftoning quantizes a grayscale or color image into one bit per pixel. There are mainly three existing methods [1], i.e., error diffusion, dithering and iterative methods (DBS). Most error diffusion halftones use *an error diffusion kernel* to minimize local weighted errors introduced by quantization. The error caused by quantizing a pixel into bi-levels is diffused into the next-processing neighbour pixels, according to the weights of the diffusion kernel. The two popular error diffusion kernels are those of Jarvis [14] and Floyd and Steinberg [15]. Most error filters have coefficients that sum to one, which guarantee that the entire system would be stable.

Most of the embedding methods use standard error diffusion frameworks. Fu and Au's embedding approach [3] divides an image into macro blocks and one bit of watermark is embedded into each block. A halftone pixel is changed to an opposite value $1 \rightarrow 0$ or $0 \rightarrow 1$, if the embedded watermark is **0** or **1** which is opposite to the image value. The watermark can be retrieved simply by extracting embedding locations in the halftone image. This approach is relatively straightforward. However, as the embedding bits increase in each block, the same value pixels may cause cluster, i.e., regionally white pixels(**1**) or black pixels(**0**) together. The cluster downgrades the overall image quality. Pei et al. [6] proposed a least-mean-square data hiding halftoning where the watermark was embedded into two or more halftone images by minimal-error bit searching and a LUT was used to retrieve the watermark. The goal of their approach is to increase watermark capacity rather than image quality. Wu [5] proposed a mathematical framework to optimize watermark embedding to multiple halftone images where the watermark image and host images were regarded as input vectors. The watermark were then extracted by performing binary logical operation i.e., XOR) to multiple halftone images. Guo et al. [9] proposed high quality progressive coding for watermarking dithered halftone image. Their method did not provide better image quality than Fu and Au's method.

In this paper we propose a method which takes into account the effects of watermarking embedding on the error diffusion halftoning process. Our goal is to build a mathematic analysis to answer why the watermarking in error diffusion process impacts the image quality and how to compensate it to preserve image perceptual quality.

3   Analysis of Halftoning Distortion in Data Hiding Error Diffusion

In this section, we analyze the key effects of sharpening and noise during the watermarking embedding process of halftone images. Idle tones also will be discussed in Section 5.1

3.1   Sharpening Problems in Data Hiding Error Diffusion

Knox [16] analyzed the quantization error in halftoning at each pixel, which is correlated with the input image. He found that the quantization error was the key reason causing annoying artifacts and *worms* in halftoning. Although worms can be reduced, the sharpness of halftone increases as the correlation of the error image with the input image increases. Sharpening distortion affects perceptual quality of the halftone image [12]. On the other hand, toggling halftone pixels in data hiding error diffusion may increase the quantization errors. Thus, the perceptual quality of image cannot be preserved.

To better model a halftone quantizer, Kite et al. [12] introduced a linear gain plus additive noise model, and applied it to error diffusion quantizer. We summarize his model as follows.

Let $x(i, j)$ is the grayscale image input and $e(i, j)$ is the quantization error caused by the quantizer output $Q(*)$ minus the quantizer input $x'(i, j)$. H(z) is the error diffusion kernel which diffuses the quantization error into neighbor pixels. A standard error diffusion can be expressed as

$$e(i, j) = y_0(i, j) - x'(i, j) \tag{1}$$
$$x'(i, j) = x(i, j) - h(i, j) * e(i, j) \tag{2}$$
$$y_0(i, j) = Q(x'(i, j)) \tag{3}$$

A quantizer output $y_0(i, j) = Q(x'(i, j))$ can be modeled as

$$Q(x'(i, j) = K_s x'(i, j) + n(i, j) \tag{4}$$

where K_s is a linearization constant based on the uncorrelated white noise $n(i, j)$ assumption. The value of K_s at any pixel is given by the ratio of the output of the quantizer to its input. Because the input to the quantizer may vary over a finite range, the output is binary, K_s varies with the input [12]. The K_s can be predicted by minimizing the square error between the halftone and model output shown in Equation (5). Based on Kite et al.'s theoretical analysis [12], $K_s \in [1, \infty]$. The visual quality of halftone image will be preserved if $K_s x'(i, j)$ is approaching halftone output infinitely, i.e., minimizing the squared error between halftone and halftone linear gain model outputs as a criterion:

$$\min_{K_s} \sum_{i,j} (K_s x'(i,j) - y(i,j))^2 \qquad (5)$$

Equations (4) and (5) will be true under the circumstance of the uncorrelated white noise assumption of residual image.

In data hiding error diffusion halftoning, we adapt Kite et al. [12] error diffusion process and combine it with watermarking embedding. We begin by specifying K_w as a linear gain in Figure 1 (K_s represents a linear gain for standard halftone [12]) and proposed a multiplicative parameter L_w compensating input image during data hiding error diffusion process as follows

$$e(i,j) = y(i,j) - x'(i,j) \qquad (6)$$
$$x'(i,j) = x(i,j) - h(i,j) * e(i,j) \qquad (7)$$
$$x''(i,j) = x'(i,j) + L_w x(i,j) \qquad (8)$$
$$y_0(i,j) = Q(x''(i,j)) \qquad (9)$$
$$y(i,j) = R(y_0(i,j)) \qquad (10)$$

where $R(*)$ in the Equation (10) represents the watermarking self-toggle quantizer. We substitute $K_w x'(i,j)$ into quantizer output $y(i,j)$ as a data hiding

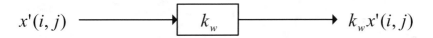

$$x'(i,j) \longrightarrow \boxed{k_w} \longrightarrow k_w x'(i,j)$$

Fig. 1. Data hiding error diffusion linear gain model

error diffusion linear gain model. By adjusting a multiplicative parameter L_w, the signal linear gain model output $K_w x'(i,j)$ would approach to watermarked halftone output infinitely, i.e., minimizing the criterion (5) with K_s replaced by K_w. However, K_w can not be estimated by the criterion (5) as long as a watermarked halftone $y(i,j)$ is obtained. But we can map K_w to standard halftone linear gain K_s in Section 3.2.

Now we use Lena image and Jarvis kernel error diffusion as examples to illustrate how L_w could be useful to reduce the correlation between the residual error image and input image(original). The correlation can be quantified as correlation coefficient [17].

$$C_{EI} = \frac{|COV[EI]|}{\sigma_E \sigma_I} \qquad (11)$$

Where σ_E and σ_I are the standard deviation of residual image E and input image I, and COV[EI] is the covariance matrix between them. The residual error images (halftone - original) for Fu and Au method and our proposed method are analyzed in Figure 2.

(a) Lena image

(b) Our proposed watermarked Lena image with 10080 bits embedded, K_w=2.0771

(c) Fu and Au's method residual error image,corr=0.0238

(d) Our proposed method's residual error image,corr=0.0110,K_w=2.0771

Fig. 2. Watermarked Halftone and Residual Error Images

Both Fu and Au's method and our proposed method embedded a binary image logo. In our case, the University of Surrey logo (90*112) [18] was used. Figure 2(a) is original Lena image. Figure 2(b) is watermarked halftone lena image based on our proposed method. Figure 2(c) is the residual error image (embedded halftone - original) based on Fu and Au's method. This residual image shows the correlation between the residual image with the input image (corr=0.0238) during data hiding error diffusion. Figure 2(d) represents our residual image based on our embedding model. From the above figures, we observe in our proposed method the residual image is approximately representing the noise (corr=0.0110). This correlation is significantly reduced as compared to Fu and Au's method. Thus, according to our experiments the sharpness of a watermarked halftone image decreases as the correlation reduces.

3.2   Determine K_w for Data Hiding Error Diffusion

In this section, we derive the mapping from K_w to K_s. Here K_s can be estimated from a standard error diffusion kernel [12]. We consider the embedding of watermark into a block-based halftoning process based on Fu and Au's method. The watermark embedding locations are determined via a Gaussian random variable. As a result, the watermark sequences become white noise embedded into the halftone image. However, due to self-toggling, the watermark bit $w(i,j)$ (0 or 1) can change the pixels in the original halftone image at the selected embedding locations of standard halftone output $y_0(i,j)$(1 or 0) in the host image. We have developed two cases for the embedding procedure.

Case 1: Embedded bit $w(i,j) = y_0(i,j)$. Let a linear gain K_w represents data hiding error diffusion linear gain. The best case scenario is that all watermark bits equal to the standard halftone output $y_0(i,j)$. In this case, none of pixel $y_0(i,j)$ will be toggled. We can simplify by taking $K_w = K_s$ corresponding with $L_w = L_s$ to reduce the sharpening of original halftone.

Case 2: Embedded bit $w(i,j) \neq y_0(i,j)$. The worst case scenario is that all standard halftone outputs $y_0(i,j)$ have to be changed. In this case, the watermarked halftone output $y(i,j)$ becomes $1 - y_0(i,j)$. Our watermarked error diffusion process is described in Equation (6) to Equation (10).

We can simply Equation (10) as follow:

$$y(i,j) = 1 - y_0(i,j) \tag{12}$$

By taking z-transformation to Equations (6-10), we obtain the Equation (13)(the detailed derivation of Equations see Appendix).

$$L_w = \frac{1 - K_w}{K_w} \tag{13}$$

Equation (13) establishes the mapping from K_w to L_w.

Now we derive the linear gain K_w for data hiding error diffusion mapped to K_s. Using the watermarking linear gain $K_w x'(i,j)$ to reach the watermarked halftone output $y(i,j)$, this can be realized by minimizing the squared error between watermarked halftone and linear gain model output as indicated in Equation (14).

$$\min_{K_w} \sum_{i,j} (K_w x'(i,j) - y(i,j))^2 \tag{14}$$

In data hiding error diffusion, the criterion (5) can be approximated with an infinite small real number $\delta_1 \geq 0$ for the watermarking linear gain model:

$$|K_w x'(i,j) - y(i,j)| = \delta_1 \tag{15}$$

By relaxing the absolute value of Equation (15) (we know watermarked halftone $y(i,j) \in [0,1]$) , we obtain

$$K_w x'(i,j) = y(i,j) + \delta_1 \tag{16}$$

Recall in case 1, in order to minimize (5) for standard halftone linear gain K_s, we derive (17) with a small real number $\delta_2 \geq 0$

$$K_s x'(i,j) - y_0(i,j) = \delta_2 \tag{17}$$

Recall in case 2, replace $y(i,j)$ in Equation (5) with (12), and a small real value $\delta_3 \geq 0$, and relax absolute value, we obtain

$$K_s x'(i,j) + y_0(i,j) = 1 + \delta_3 \tag{18}$$

Combine (17) and (18), we obtain

$$2K_s x'(i,j) = 1 + \delta_2 + \delta_3 \tag{19}$$

From (16) and (19), for halftone image $|y(i,j)| \leq 1$, we obtain

$$\frac{K_w x'(i,j)}{2K_s x'(i,j)} = \frac{y(i,j) + \delta_1}{1 + \delta_2 + \delta_3} \leq 1 \tag{20}$$

Therefore, we derive $K_w \leq 2K_s$. The watermarked halftone linear gain can be represented by $K_w \in [K_s, 2K_s]$. As we mentioned K_w cannot be obtained without a watermark embedded. Each watermark embedded in the halftone image has a unique K_w value that can minimize the criterion $\sum_{i,j}(K_w x'(i,j) - y(i,j))^2$. This minimization is achieved by our proposed iterative linear gain model as described in section 4.

4   Iterative Linear Gain for Watermarking Error Diffusion

In Section 3, we analyzed sharpening distortion in data hiding error diffusion. In this section, we propose our visual quality preserving algorithm for data hiding error diffusion via iterative linear gain for watermarking halftone. By adjusting a multiplicative parameter L_w to compensate the input image in data hiding halftoning, the sharpening distortion decreases as the correlation between original image and residual image decreases. Thus, we can obtain the least distortion watermarked halftone image. This results in our proposed iterative linear gain model for optimum perceptual image quality of halftone images as illustrated in Figure 3.

4.1   Iterative Data Hiding Error Diffusion Algorithm

We found that the greater linear gain K_w the lesser the sharpening and harmonic distortion. To accurately measure a perceptual quality of a halftone image, Kite et al. [12] proposed the use of weighted SNR (WSNR) for the subjective quality measure of halftone image. WSNR weights the Signal-to-Noise Ratio (SNR) according to the contrast sensitivity function (CSF) of the human visual system. For an image of size $M \times N$ pixels, WSNR is defined as

$$WSNR(dB) = 10\log_{10}\left(\frac{\sum_{u,v}|(X(u,v)C(u,v)|^2}{\sum_{u,v}|(X(u,v) - Y(u,v)C(u,v)|^2}\right) \tag{21}$$

where $X(u,v), Y(u,v)$, and $C(u,v)$ represent the Discrete Fourier Transforms (DFT's) of the input image, output image, and CSF, respectively, and $0 \leq u \leq M-1$ and $0 \leq v \leq N-1$. With WSNR, we optimize K_w to minimize the halftone watermarking image distortion. In Section 3, as the K_w increases, the correlation between residual error image and input image is reduced. We use an iterative approach to find the best K_w for maximum WSNR of embedded halftone image. In this way, we can find the least distortion halftone watermarking image. Based on this concept, our new halftone embedding process is illustrated in Figure 3. The embedding process first divides an image into macro blocks. Each macro block embeds one bit. Toggling halftone pixels is the same as Fu and Au's method [3] so that if the bit of watermark is the same as the original halftone pixel, no action is taken. If the watermark bit is different from the halftone pixel, then the bit is toggled.

However, K_w can only be determined if a watermark is embedded, which is a random combination between 0 and 1. Thus, in Section 4 we inferred our estimation of K_w from the Case one and Case two based on the estimation of K_s. We concluded $K_w \in [K_s, 2K_s]$. In our algorithm, K_w is selected by starting from K_s, and the algorithm iterates by adding one additive amount b, i.e., $b = 0.2$ to K_w in each loop. It generates corresponding halftone image measured by WSNR. We measured K_w empirically using five test images and results are shown in Figure 4. It is found as the K_w varies the WSNR increases until it peakes at the point. Our K_w starts from K_s and increased by step of 0.2. The K_w varies within $[K_s, 2K_s]$. The corresponding WSNR is computed. Once the maximum WSNR value is found, the iteration will then terminates.

The calculation of WSNR is shown in Equation (21), where $X(u,v)$ is the input image shown as the numerator, $Y(u,v)$ is output image, $X(u,v) - Y(u,v)$ shown as the denominator which presents the noise image. The maximum WSNR will be found when the denominator in Equation (21) is infinitely small. It is similar to the process of minimizing the quantization noise (the differential between output and input) shown in Equation (14). However, the quantization noise will never be zero or equivalent to white noise. Otherwise the denominator in Equation (14) will be

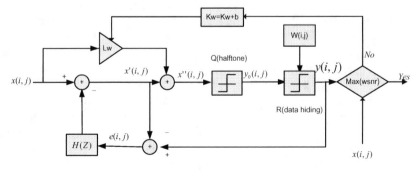

Fig. 3. Iterative linear gain halftone embedding

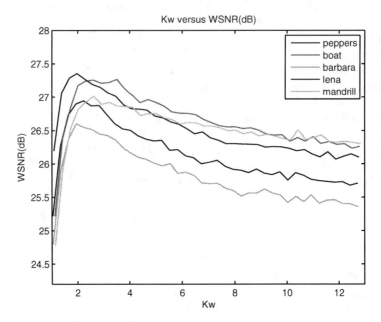

Fig. 4. The relationship between K_w and WSNR

Table 1. Iteration numbers

loop step	peppers	boat	barbara	lena	mandrill
0.2	8	8	7	6	9
0.3	6	7	5	5	7

equal to zero. We simulated the WSNR variation with an increase of K_w presented in Figure 4. Each image in Figure 4 has a peak value of WSNR corresponding to a unique K_w which minimizes the criterion indicated in Equation (14). As noticed, for boat image, there is another peak value after the first. It is because the Equation (14) is an approximated value. Its quantization noise may be not pure white noise. This exceptional value doesn't affect the algorithm to find the best possible quality of image.

The mathematics proof of explicit relationship between $K_w(K_s)$ and WSNR can not be provided at this stage. But it would be interesting to explore in the future.

The complexity of our iterative algorithm is $O(1)$ because our algorithm will terminate once the first maximum WSNR has been found in the iteration. The maximum point defines as the current WSNR greater than the next value of WSNR. In our theoretical analysis, the K_w value is estimated as $[K_s, 2K_s]$. Even when the iterative step is very small, the iteration number will be limited when the maximum WSNR is found subject to the Equation 14. The iteration number for each test image has been recorded and presented in Table 1.

5   Experiments and Results Analysis

Modified Peak Signal-to-Noise Ratio (MPSNR) [3] and Weighted Signal-to-noise Ratio(WSNR) [12] have been commonly used for evaluating halftone image quality. However, one main disadvantage of MPSNR is that it only compares the original image with the watermarked halftone image. The watermarked halftone image first undergos a Gaussian low-pass filter while the original image still contains high frequency components. This results in the inaccurate calculation of SNR because errors are incurred due to high frequency components remained in the grayscale image.

Our experiments were performed on five images with different sizes of watermark embedded using The University of Surrey logo in Jarvis kernel. Each experiment uses the same embedding locations and different watermark sizes. Figure 2(b) is lena halftone image with 10080 bits (90*112) embedded at K_w=2.077 with WSNR=27.37 (dB). We use WSNR metric for subjective quality comparison of watermarked halftone quality as given in Table 2 and MPSNR in Table 3. From Table 2, our approach has an average improvement of 6.5% over Fu and Au's method. MPSNR measure shows that our approach is slightly higher than Fu and Au's method except for the image mandrill and barbara in high capacity embedding. This may be caused by the fact that both mandrill and barbara contained some high frequency components.

Figure 5 illustrates the results of applying our proposed method and Fu and Au's method data hiding error diffusion to five test images. From this figure, we conclude our approach can preserve the high quality of watermarked halftone with different sizes of watermark embedded. Overall Fu and Au's method cannot maintain the WSNR as good as our method for different host images. This is due

Table 2. WSNR Comparison Between Our's Method and Fu and Au's Method (dB)

mark size	32x32		64x64		90x90		90x112		Avg. Impr.%
image	our	Fu & Au	our	Fu & Au	our	Fu & Au	our	Fu & Au	our impr.
peppers	27.643	25.273	27.380	25.164	27.073	25.098	26.936	25.068	8.392
boat	27.582	24.674	27.533	24.673	27.231	24.609	27.112	24.570	11.470
barbara	27.224	24.923	27.133	24.825	26.778	24.669	26.558	24.585	8.734
lena	27.729	26.038	27.618	25.920	27.449	25.868	27.375	25.830	6.565
mandrill	27.222	24.116	27.066	24.094	26.972	24.076	26.909	24.005	12.474

Table 3. MPSNR Comparison Between Our's Method and Fu and Au's Method (dB)

mark size	32x32		64x64		90x90		90x112	
image	our	Fu and Au	our	Fu and Au	our	Fu and Au	our	Fu and Au
peppers	27.168	26.729	26.958	26.567	26.705	26.429	26.601	26.327
boat	26.048	25.710	25.965	25.651	25.733	25.455	25.598	25.404
barbara	24.095	24.078	23.998	23.997	23.844	23.856	23.772	23.785
lena	27.017	26.917	26.895	26.783	26.701	26.653	26.623	26.560
mandrill	22.620	22.724	22.581	22.670	22.505	22.620	22.463	22.572

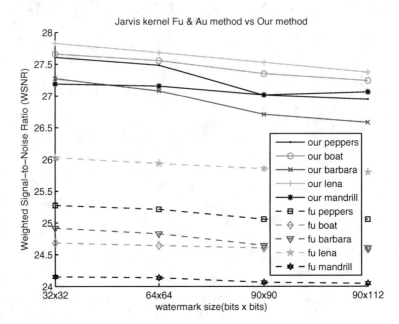

Fig. 5. WSNR of Fu method vs Our method

to our iterative linear gain model can effectively compensate the watermarking effects during halftone error diffusion process.

Figure 6 illustrates the percentage of improvement of our method over Fu and Au's method. Even for the worst case image *lena*, our method achieved an improvement of approximately 6-7% compared to Fu and Au's method. The other watermarked halftone images are shown in Figure 9.

Furthermore, the latest visual quality evaluation called *visual information fidelity (VIF)* [19] was proposed to use human visual system (HVS) model for image quality assessment (QA). VIF is a model for distortion (22) and can be used to quantify the loss of image information to the distortion process and explore the relationship between image information and visual quality. We use it to compare the loss of image distortion between different watermarking halftone images. Table 4 are measured results for both Fu and An's method and our method. These results show that our model have $11\% - 23\%$ improvement than Fu and Au's method. This confirms the effectiveness of our iterative linear gain model in data hiding error diffusion so as to achieve the least distortion image.

$$VIF = \frac{\sum(subbands\ of\ wavelet\ coefficients\ in\ distorted\ image)}{\sum(subbands\ of\ wavelet\ coefficients\ in\ reference\ image)} \quad (22)$$

5.1   Tonality Validation in Watermarked Halftone Image

Idle tones appears as strong cycle patterns. Idle tones affect the quality of halftone. Kite et.al [12] analogized the halftone distortion, which was caused

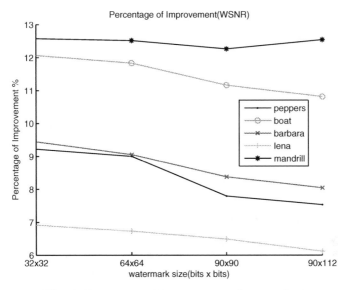

Fig. 6. Percentage of improvement of our method

Table 4. VIF Comparison Between Our's Method and Fu and Au's Method

mark size	32x32		64x64		90x90		90x112		VIF comp.		
image	our	Fu	our	Fu	our	Fu	our	Fu	our avg.	Fu avg.	Impr. (%)
peppers	0.2519	0.2165	0.2551	0.2125	0.2413	0.2066	0.2405	0.2075	0.2472	0.2108	17.2753
boat	0.2534	0.2004	0.2467	0.1995	0.2407	0.1968	0.2380	0.1959	0.2447	0.1981	23.5004
barbara	0.2494	0.2208	0.2411	0.2175	0.2336	0.2105	0.2306	0.2083	0.2387	0.2143	11.3768
lena	0.2456	0.2108	0.2425	0.2092	0.2418	0.2044	0.2345	0.2043	0.2411	0.2072	16.3821
mandrill	0.2242	0.1882	0.2250	0.1866	0.2227	0.1845	0.2201	0.1838	0.2230	0.1858	20.0365

by idle tone, with total harmonic distortion. By computing the power spectral density of watermarking halftone, we propose our method to adapt to the *total harmonic distortion* [13] for analyzing tonality, i.e. the signal power distribution over frequencies. The power spectral density (PSD), describes how the power (or variance) of a time series is distributed with frequency. Mathematically, it is defined as the Fourier Transform of the autocorrelation sequence of the time series. Let x is the signal of halftone image, the PSD is the Fourier transform of the autocorrelation function, $autocorr(\tau)$, of the signal if the signal can be treated as a stationary random process,

$$S(x) = \int_{-\infty}^{\infty} autocorr(\tau) \, e^{-2\pi i x \tau} \, d\tau. \tag{23}$$

$$PSD = \int_{F_1}^{F_2} S(x) \, dx + \int_{-F_2}^{-F_1} S(x) \, dx. \tag{24}$$

where the power of the signal in a given frequency band can be calculated in (24) by integrating over positive and negative frequencies.

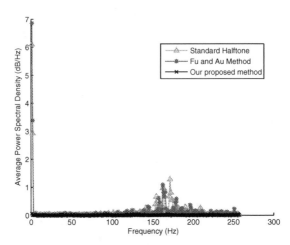

Fig. 7. Average Power Spectral Density of halftone boat images

The spectral density is usually estimated using Welch's method [20], where we define a Hann window to sample the signal x. To this end, we define the average PSD under a Hann window of 512 samples (two-side 256 sample dots)as

$$\overline{PSD} = \frac{1}{257}PSD. \tag{25}$$

For the Jarvis kernel, we embedded the surrey logo(90x112 bits) into the image *boat* of sizes 512x512. For $\overline{PSD}$ comparison, we analyzed the tonality of our proposed watermarking model compared with Fu and Au's method. The $\overline{PSD}$s of image *boat* are illustrated in Figure 7. As described in Section 3, our proposed model reduces the tonality of watermarked halftone images by adaptively adjusting K_w. This figure shows that Fu and Au's method(red line) generated higher $\overline{PSD}$ than the original halftone (green line). However, our method (blue line, while K_w=2.514) achieved $\overline{PSD}$ much smoother than the others. The same experiments were performed to all five images, and measured average power spectral desnity ($\overline{PSD}$) to all five images, as shown in Table 5. Where the K_w^1 in Table 5 is the initial value of K_w and the last K_w^{opt} is the optimum value of K_w. We found that image peppers's halftone has zero $\overline{PSD}$. This means its autocorrelation function is zero. However, when a watermark was embedded, it introduced harmonic distortion. The $\overline{PSD}$ for watermarked image peppers was approximately 0.0096 (dB/Hz) for both Fu and Au's method and our proposed method. Based on our model, we also found that the overall $\overline{PSD}$ of five images was reduced as K_w increased until it reached approximately $2K_w^1$. For example, image *boat*'s $\overline{PSD}$ reduces from 0.0893 (dB/Hz) (K_w^1=1.114) to 0.0096 (dB/Hz)(K_w^{opt}=2.514). We conclude that the lower the value and more uniformly distributed the $\overline{PSD}$, the lower would be the harmonic distortion. By finding an optimum K_w, the least distorted watermarked halftone image is

Table 5. Average Power Spectral Density

image	halftone	Fu and Au method	our proposed method (dB/Hz)	
peppers	0	0.0096	$0.0096(K_w^1{=}1.035)$	$0.0096(K_w^{opt}{=}2.435)$
boat	0.1053	0.1122	$0.0893(K_w^1{=}1.114)$	$0.0096(K_w^{opt}{=}2.514)$
barbara	0.2225	0.2185	$0.2153(K_w^1{=}1.045)$	$0.1071(K_w^{opt}{=}2.445)$
lena	0.0535	0.0521	$0.0507(K_w^1{=}1.077)$	$0.0099(K_w^{opt}{=}2.477)$
mandrill	0.1796	0.1914	$0.1632(K_w^1{=}1.132)$	$0.0322(K_w^{opt}{=}2.532)$

obtained. Therefore, an optimum perceptual quality is preserved via minimizing distortion in the data hiding error diffusion halftone images.

6 Conclusion

In this paper, we analyzed the perceptual distortion of watermarking embedding in error diffusion of halftone image. Two major impacts generated by data hiding error diffusion of halftone images have been clarified as: Firstly, sharpening distortion, as a consequence of the quantization error image being correlated with original grayscale image in the standard data hiding error diffusion; Secondly, the error diffused by *an error diffusion kernel* is distributed directionally in standard data hiding error diffusion process. It causes tonality, which results in strong cycle patterns. From our mathematical framework, we proposed the linear gain model for data hiding error diffusion halftoning and derived our optimized linear gain parameter K_w by mapping it to the halftoning linear gain model K_s. Theoretically, the K_w value has been estimated to be in the range of $[K_s, 2K_s]$. The increase of K_w towards variation of image quality quantified by WSNR was measured empirically using test images and results were presented. The optimum watermarked halftone image was found by choosing the maximum WSNR value. This model minimizes a significant amount of distortion resulting in 6.5% to 12% improvement of WSNR and 11% to 23% improvement of VIF, which finalized an embedded halftone image to be unsharpened and quantization error approximating an uncorrelated Gaussian white noise. This model adopted an iterative approach to minimizing the impacts of distortion in the data hiding error diffusion process without introducing the complexity $O(1)$. This minimized the differences between the grayscale image and the embedded halftone image. Consequently, the perceptual quality for halftone watermark embedding was found to be better than Fu and Au's method in terms of WSNR and VIF. The proposed linear gain control model was also validated using an average power spectral density.

Our future work will focus on robust watermarking approach for halftone image using error correction coding. Moreover, authentication and restoration will also be investigated.

Acknowledgments

We would like to thank Dr. Thomas D. Kite and Prof. Brian L. Evans from the University of Texas for their invaluable advice. We would like to acknowledge the comments and feedback from the reviewers, which help to improve this paper further.

References

1. Ulichney, R.: Digital Halftoning. MIT Press, Cambridge (1987)
2. Petitcolas, F., Anderson, R., Kuhn, M.: Information hiding-a survey. IEEE Proceedings 87(7), 1062–1078 (1999)
3. Fu, M.S., Au, O.C.: Data hiding watermarking for halftone images. IEEE Transactions on Image Processding 11(4) (2002)
4. Phil Sherry, A.S.: Improved techniques for watermarking halftone images. In: IEEE International Conference on Acoustics Speech and Signal Processing, vol. 8, pp. V1005–V1008 (2004)
5. Wu, C.W., Thompson, G., Stanich, M.: Digital watermarking and steganography via overlays of halftone images. Ibm research report, IBM Research Division,Thomas J. Watson Research Center, P.O. Box 218,Yorktown Heights, NY 10598 (2004)
6. Soo-Chang Pei, J.M.G.: High-capacity data hiding in halftone images using minimal-error bit searching and least-mean square filter. IEEE Transactions on Image Processing 15(6) (2006)
7. Baharav, Z., Shaked, D.: Watermarking of dither halftoned images. In: IS&T/SPIE Int. Conf. Security Watermark, Multimedia content 3657, pp. 307–316 (1999)
8. Hel-Or, H.: Watermarking and copyright labeling of printed images. J. Electron. Imaging 10(3), 794–803 (2001)
9. Guo, J.M., Pei, S.C., Lee, H.: Paired subimage matching watermarking method on ordered dither images and its high-quality progressive coding. IEEE Transactions on Multimedia 10(1) (2008)
10. Kacker, D., Allebach, J.P.: Joint halftoning and watermarking. IEEE Transactions on Signal Processing 51(4) (2003)
11. Hsieh, C.T., Lu, Y.L., Luo, C.P., Kuo, F.J.: A study of enhancing the robustness of watermark. In: Proceedings of International Symposium on Multimedia Software Engineering, pp. 325–327 (2000)
12. Kite, T.D., Evans, B.L., Bovik, A.C.: Modeling and quality assessment of halftoning by error diffusion. IEEE Transactions on Image Processing 9(5) (2000)
13. Horowitz, P., Hill, W.: The art of Eletronics. Cambridge Univ. Press, Cambridge (1980)
14. Jarvis, J., Judice, C., Ninke, W.: A survey of techniques for the display of continuous tone pictures on bilevel displays. In: Comp. Graph. and Image Proc., vol. 5, pp. 13–40 (1976)
15. Floyd, R., Steinberg, L.: An adaptive algorithm for spatial grayscale. Proceedings of the Society for Information Display 17(2), 75–77 (1976)
16. Knox, K.: Error image in error diffusion. In: SPIE, Image Processing Algorithms and Techniques III, vol. 1657, pp. 268–279 (1992)
17. Williams, R.: Electrical Engineering Probability, 1st edn. West, St. Paul (1991)

18. University of S.: Surrey logo (2007), http://www.surrey.ac.uk/assets/images/surreylogo.gif
19. Hamid Rahim Sheikh, A.C.B.: Image information and visual quality. IEEE Transactions on Image Processsding 15(2) (2006)
20. Lfeachor, E.C., Jervis, B.W.: Digital Signal Processing: A Practical Approach, 1st edn. Addison-Wesley, Reading (1993)

Appendix A

This appendix is derivation of the Equation L_w. In [12], the standard error diffusion transfer equation with signal transform function and noise transform function, can be expressed as z-transformation

$$Y(z) = \underbrace{\frac{K_s}{1 + (K_s - 1)H(z)}}_{STF} X(z) + \frac{1 - H(z)}{1 + (K_n - 1)H(z)} N(z) \qquad (26)$$

Replace Equation (12) into Equations (6) and (10). We obtain:

$$e(i,j) = 1 - y_0(i,j) - x'(i,j) \qquad (27)$$
$$x'(i,j) = x(i,j) - h(i,j) * e(i,j) \qquad (28)$$
$$x''(i,j) = x'(i,j) + L_w x(i,j) \qquad (29)$$
$$y_0(i,j) = Q(x''(i,j)) \qquad (30)$$
$$y(i,j) = 1 - y_0(i,j) \qquad (31)$$

Substituting $x'(i,j)$ in Equation (28) into Equation (29), and taking z transform, we have

$$X''(z) = (1 + L_w)X(z) - H(z)E(z) \qquad (32)$$

From Equation (27) and Equation (28), taking the z transform, we have

$$E(z) = \frac{\frac{Z}{Z-1} - Y_0(z) - X(z)}{1 - H(z)} \qquad (33)$$

From Equation (32) and Equation (33), we derive

$$X''(z) = [1 + L_w + \frac{H(z)}{1 - H(z)}]X(z) + \frac{H(z)}{1 - H(z)}Y_0(z) - \frac{Z}{Z-1}\frac{H(z)}{1 - H(z)} \qquad (34)$$

In Figure 8, we draw the equivalent modified circuit to watermarking linear gain model. we obtain

$$e(i,j) = 1 - y_0(i,j) - x''(i,j) \qquad (35)$$
$$x''(i,j) = g(i,j) * x(i,j) - h(i,j) * e(i,j) \qquad (36)$$
$$y_0(i,j) = Q(x''(i,j)) \qquad (37)$$
$$y(i,j) = 1 - y_0(i,j) \qquad (38)$$

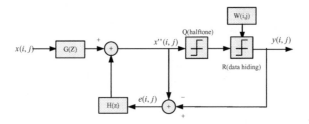

Fig. 8. Equivalent modified circuit

where $g(i, j)$ is an impulse response of G(z). From Equation (35) and Equation (36), we have

$$E(z) = \frac{\frac{Z}{Z-1} - Y_0(z) - G(z)X(z)}{1 - H(z)} \tag{39}$$

we substitute Equation (39) into the z-transform of Equation (36) ,we derive

$$X''(z) = [G(z) + \frac{G(z)H(z)}{1 - H(z)}]X(z) + \frac{H(z)}{1 - H(z)}Y_0(z) - \frac{Z}{Z-1}\frac{H(z)}{1 - H(z)} \tag{40}$$

Equation (34) is equal to Equation (40),when

$$1 + L + \frac{H(z)}{1 - H(z)} = G(z) + \frac{G(z)H(z)}{1 - H(z)} \tag{41}$$

Then, we obtain

$$G(z) = 1 + [1 - H(z)]L_w \tag{42}$$

If we compare Equation (42) with the Signal Transform Function expressed in Equation (26),in which the watermarked halftone image with linear gain K_w has the same signal transfer function, G(z) can be expressed as the reciprocal of the STF. Thus,

$$L_w = \frac{1 - K_w}{K_w} \tag{43}$$

□

(a) our watermarked boat image, K_w=2.514

(b) our watermarked peppers image, K_w=2.435

(c) our watermarked barbara image, K_w=2.445

(d) our watermarked mandrill image, K_w=2.532

Fig. 9. Watermarked Halftone Images with Surreylogo 10080 bits embedded

Optimum Histogram Pair Based Image Lossless Data Embedding*

Guorong Xuan[1], Yun Q. Shi[2], Peiqi Chai[1], Jianzhong Teng[1],
Zhicheng Ni[3], and Xuefeng Tong[1]

[1] Dept. of Computer Science, Tongji University, Shanghai, China
grxuan@public1.sta.net.cn
[2] Dept. of ECE, New Jersey Institute of Technology, Newark, New Jersey, USA
shi@njit.edu
[3] LSI Corporation, Allentown, Pennsylvania, USA

Abstract. This paper presents an optimum histogram pair based image reversible data hiding scheme using integer wavelet transform and adaptive histogram modification. This new scheme is characterized by (1) the selection of best threshold T, which leads to the highest PSNR of marked image for a given payload; (2) the adaptive histogram modification, which aims at avoiding underflow and/or overflow, is carried out only when it is necessary, and treats the left side and right side of histogram individually, seeking a minimum amount of histogram modification; and (3) the selection of most suitable embedding region, which attempts to further improve the PSNR of marked image in particular when the payload is low. Consequently, to our best knowledge, it can achieve the highest visual quality of marked image for a given payload as compared with the prior arts of image reversible data hiding. The experimental results have been presented to confirm the claimed superior performance.

Keywords: optimum histogram pair, reversible (lossless) data embedding, integer wavelets, selection of best threshold, adaptive histogram modification, selection of suitable embedding region.

1 Introduction

Reversible data embedding, also often called lossless data hiding, requires that not only hidden data can be extracted correctly but also the marked image be inverted back to the original cover image exactly after the hidden data has been extracted out. Recently, Ni et al. [1] proposed the reversible data embedding algorithm based on the spatial domain histogram shifting. Tian[2] proposed the difference expansion method that can achieve a high payload, but it can only be used with integer Haar wavelet. Kamstra and Heijmans[3] improved the PSNR of marked image achieved by Tian in the case of small payload.

---

* This research is supported partly by National Natural Science Foundation of China (NSFC) on the project (90304017).

Y.Q. Shi (Ed.): Transactions on DHMS IV, LNCS 5510, pp. 84–102, 2009.

Xuan et al.[4] proposed the thresholding reversible embedding using the integer wavelet transform (IWT) and histogram modification. In [5], some improvements over [4] have been made about the selection of threshold. However, the three optimality measures taken in this paper have not been developed in [5]. In [6], Yang et al. applied the histogram shifting embedding to the integer discrete cosine transform. The reversible data hiding scheme proposed in this paper is based on optimum histogram pairs. It is characterized by selection of optimum threshold T; most suitable embedding region R; and minimum possible amount of histogram modification G, in order to achieve highest PSNR of the stego image for a given data embedding capacity.

The rest of this paper is organized as follows. The principle of reversible data embedding based on histogram pairs is illustrated in Section 2. Integer wavelets and histogram modification are briefly discussed in Section 3. The proposed reversible data hiding algorithm is presented in Section 4 and 5. Section 6 provides experimental results. The performance of three newest algorithms published in 2007 [7,8,9] is cited for comparison. Discussion and conclusion are presented in Section 7.

2 Principle of Histogram Pair

2.1 Reversible Data Embedding Using Histogram Pair

Histogram $h(x)$ is the number of occurrence as the variable X assumes value x. Since digital image and IWT are considered in this paper, we assume X can only assume integer values. In order to illustrate the concept of histogram pair, we first consider a very simple case. That is, only two consecutive integers a and b assumed by X are considered, i.e. $x \in \{a, b\}$. Furthermore, let $h(a) = m$ and $h(b) = 0$. We call these two points as a histogram pair, and sometimes denote it by, $h = [m, 0]$, or simply $[m, 0]$. Furthermore, we assume $m = 4$. That is, X actually assumes integer value a four times, i.e., $X = [a, a, a, a]$. Next, let's see how we can reversibly embed bits into $X = [a, a, a, a]$. Suppose the to-be-embedded binary sequence is $D = [1, 0, 0, 1]$. In data embedding, we scan the 1-D sequence $X = [a, a, a, a]$ in certain ordering, say, from left to right. When we meet the first a, since we want to embed bit 1, we change a to b. For the next two to-be-embedded bits, since they are bit 0, we do not change a. For the last to-be-embedded bit 1, we change a to b. Therefore, after the four-bit embedding, we have $X = [b, a, a, b]$, and the histogram is now $h = [2, 2]$. Embedding capacity is $C = 4$. The hidden data extraction, or histogram pair recovery, is the reverse process of data embedding: after extracting the data $D = [1, 0, 0, 1]$, the histogram pair becomes $[4, 0]$ and we can recover $X = [a, a, a, a]$ reversibly.

We define histogram pair here. If for two consecutive non-negative values a and b that X can assume, we have $h(a) = m$ and $h(b) = n$, where m and n are the numbers of occurrence for $x = a$ and $x = b$, respectively. When $n = 0$, we call $h = [m, n]$ as a histogram pair. From the above example, we observe that when $n = 0$, we can use this histogram pair to embed data reversibly. We call

Original histogram				After embedding			
h=[16,0,0,0]				h=[8,8,0,0]			
a	a	a	a	b	a	a	b
a	a	a	a	a	b	b	a
a	a	a	a	a	b	b	a
a	a	a	a	b	a	a	b
(a) original image				(b) embedding			

Fig. 1. Image and histogram for 1st loop embedding

Expansion				Embedding			
h=[8,0,8,0]				h=[4,4,4,4]			
c	a	a	c	d	a	b	c
a	c	c	a	b	c	d	a
a	c	c	a	b	c	d	a
c	a	a	c	d	a	b	c
(a) expansion				(b) embedding			

Fig. 2. Image and histogram for 2nd loop embedding

$n = 0$ in the above defined histogram pair as an "expansion" element, which is ready for reversible data embedding. During the embedding, we scan all of x values, a, in certain order. If bit 1 is to be embedded, we change the a under scanning to b, otherwise, we keep the a unchanged. If a is a negative integer, then $h = [m, n]$ is a histogram pair as $m = 0$ and $n \neq 0$.

2.2 An Illustrative Example

In this example, $D = [1, 0, 0, 1, 0, 1, 1, 0, 0, 1, 1, 0, 1, 0, 0, 1]$, a 16-bit sequence is to be embedded into a 4×4 image by using the histogram pair scheme. For this image $x \in \{a, b, c, d\}$, and a, b, c, d are four consecutive integers. Assume the image's histogram is $h = [16, 0, 0, 0]$ as shown in Figure 1(a). We noticed that the two numbers, 16 and 0 having been underlined, form a histogram pair. Let's scan the image from left to right, and from top-to-bottom. The same rule is obeyed, i.e., when bit 0 is to be embedded, a remains, when bit 1 is to be embedded, a changes to b. Figure 1 displays images and histograms before and after the first loop of data embedding, while Figure 2 for the 2nd loop embedding.

1st loop: There is one histogram pair $h = [16, 0]$ that can be used. After embedding, the histogram pair $[16, 0]$ changes to $[8, 8]$, the histogram changed from $h = [16, 0, 0, 0]$ to $h = [8, 8, 0, 0]$, see Figure 1. The scanned image pixel value sequence changes from $X = [a, a, a, a, a, a, a, a, a, a, a, a, a, a, a, a]$ to $X = [b, a, a, b, a, b, b, a, a, b, b, a, b, a, a, b]$ as shown in Figure1(b). After this loop, 16 bits have been embedded.

2nd loop: Since the resultant pair $[8, 8]$ cannot be used to embed data, we first expand the histogram by change b to c in the image, resulting in the new histogram $h = [8, 0, 8, 0]$ as shown in Figure 2. Now, there are two histogram pairs, $[8, 0]$ (left) and $[8, 0]$ (right). After data embedding, the histogram changes from $h = [8, 0, 8, 0]$ to $h = [4, 4, 4, 4]$, see Figure 2. Both histogram pairs change from $[8, 0]$ to $[4, 4]$. The scanned image pixel value sequence changes from $X = [c, a, a, c, a, c, c, a, a, c, c, a, c, a, a, c]$ to $X = [d, a, b, c, b, c, d, a, b, c, d, a, d, a, b, c]$ as shown in Figure2. After data embedding in 2nd loop, another 16 bits are embedded. In total, we have embedded 216=32 bits into this 44 image by these two loops.

2.3 Upper Bound of Data Embedding Capacity

The above example has indicated that multiple-loop embedding can embed more data. However, the embedding capacity has an upper bound. When bit 0 and bit 1 are equally distributed among the to-be-embedded sequence, the upper bound of embedding capacity can be calculated. Assume the number of image pixels (or wavelet coefficients) is N, then at most N bits can be embedded for each embedding loop. Assume the number of different x values is M. The number of loops, r, can be calculated by $r = log(M)$, i.e., $M = 2r$. Then, after r loop embedding, the capacity becomes $L = rN$. If after r loop embedding, the histogram becomes flat, it means the maximum capacity has been achieved. In the example in Section 2.2, $N = 16$, $M = 4$, hence it can embed $r = 2$ loops. After twice embedding, in the example, $h = [4, 4, 4, 4]$, i.e., histogram becomes completely horizontal, indicating no data can be embedded any more. In this case, the maximum capacity has been reached, which is $L = rN = 216 = 32$ bits.

2.4 Information Theory

Histogram expansion and data embedding will cause the histogram change from up-and-down to relatively more flat. In this way, the entropy increases. On the other hand, data extraction will lead to the opposite, and the entropy decreases to its original value. This process can be shown below.

The entropy can be expressed as $H(x) = -\int h(x) \log(h(x)) dx$. It can be proved according to information theory that the probability distribution $h(x)$ will be uniform within a limited range $u \sim v$ when the maximum entropy $H(x)$ is achieved:

$$h(x) = \arg_{h(x)} \max[H(x) - \lambda(1 - \int_u^v h(x)dx)] = \frac{1}{v - u} \quad (1)$$

Proof: If $d[H(x) - \lambda(1 - \int_u^v h(x)dx)]/dx = 0$, we have $-(1 + \log h(x)) + \lambda = 0$. Consider the condition of probability distribution $\int_u^v h(x)dx = 1$, the solution $h(x) = \frac{1}{v-u}$ is obtained.

In summary, after data embedding, the entropy increases and histogram becomes more flat. If the histogram is absolutely flat, the total entropy $H(x)$ is maximum, no more data can be embedded.

3 Integer Wavelets and Histogram Modification

3.1 Integer Wavelet Transform (IWT)

In this proposed method, data is hidden into IWT coefficients of high-frequency subbands. The motivation of doing so is as follows. (1) The high frequency subband coefficients represent the high frequency components of the image. Human visual system (HVS) is less sensitive to high frequency. Hence, data embedding into high frequency subbands can lead to better imperceptibility of marked image. (2) The histogram distribution of high-frequency subbands is Laplacian-like with a huge peak around zero. This makes high data embedding capacity feasible. (3) Owing to the de-correlation property among the wavelet subbands in the same decomposition level, data embedding using IWT results in higher PSNR than embedding into other transform coefficients such as DCT.

Due to the reversibility constraint, we choose to use integer wavelet transform. Specifically, the integer Haar wavelet transform and integer (5,3) wavelet transform are used in our experimental works. Other types of IWT are usable too. The results are shown in Section 5, from which we observe that both perform well, however, the integer (5,3) transform performs better, while the integer Haar transform is more simple in implementation.

3.2 Formulas of Wavelet Transform

Formulas for the above-mentioned two integer wavelet transforms are listed in Table 1.

Table 1. Integer wavelet transform

Type of wavelet transform		Formulas
Integer Haar wavelet transform	Forward transform	Splitting: $s_i \leftarrow x_{2i}; d_i \leftarrow x_{2i+1}$ Dual lifting: $d_i \leftarrow d_i - s_i$ Primary lifting: $s_i \leftarrow s_i + \lfloor d_i/2 + (1/2) \rfloor$
	Inverse transform	Inverse primary lifting: $s_i \leftarrow s_i - \lfloor d_i/2 + (1/2) \rfloor$ Inverse dual lifting: $d_i \leftarrow d_i + s_i$ Merging: $x_{2i} \leftarrow s_i; x_{2i+1} \leftarrow d_i$
Integer (5,3) wavelet transform	Forward transform	Splitting: $s_i \leftarrow x_{2i}; d_i \leftarrow x_{2i+1}$ Dual lifting: $d_i \leftarrow d_i - \lfloor (s_i + s_{i+1})/2 + (1/2) \rfloor$ Primary lifting: $s_i \leftarrow s_i - \lfloor (d_{i-1} + d_i)/4 + (1/2) \rfloor$
	Inverse transform	Inverse primary lifting: $s_i \leftarrow s_i - \lfloor (d_{i-1}/2 + d_i)/4 + (1/2) \rfloor$ Inverse dual lifting: $d_i \leftarrow d_i + \lfloor (s_i + s_{i+1})/2 + (1/2) \rfloor$ Merging: $x_{2i} \leftarrow s_i; x_{2i+1} \leftarrow d_i$

Note that $\lfloor x \rfloor$ rounds x to the largest integer not larger than x.

3.3 Histogram Modification

For a given image, after data embedding into some IWT coefficients, it is possible to cause *underflow* and/or *overflow*, which means that the grayscale values may exceed the range [0, 255] for an 8-bit gray image, thus possibly violating the losslessness constraint. In order to prevent this from happening, we adjust histogram, i.e., we shrink the histogram from one or both sides towards the central portion. In narrowing down a histogram, we need to record the histogram modification for late recovery of the original image, thus resulting in bookkeeping data, which is to be embedded into the image as a part of the actually embedded data. Instead of adjust histogram as a preprocessing as done in [4] and [5] (meaning that histogram modification is always done at the beginning no matter if necessary or not), we do it only when this is necessary (meaning that the adjustment is done adaptively in data embedding when it is necessary), furthermore the left side and right side of histogram is treated individually. More discussion in this regard will be given below.

If the overflow occurs (at the right side, i.e., the grayscale value is larger than 255), the right end of the histogram will be shrunk towards the center by an amount GR. If the underflow occurs (at the left side, i.e., the grayscale value is smaller than 0), the left end of the histogram will be shrunk towards the center by an amount GL. Together, the histogram is shrunk by an amount of G, and $G = GL + GR$. The histogram is narrowed down from "0 to 255" to "GL to $(255 - GR)$". This histogram shrinking uses the histogram pair principle described above as well, specifically it is the reverse process of data embedding (which expands the histogram). This new dynamic way contributes to the superior performance over that of [4] and [5] and will be shown in Sections 5 and 6. There, it is observed that it may not need to do histogram modification for some images with some payloads. When the embedding capacity increases, we may need histogram modification. In addition, the amount of histogram modification for the right side and the left side of histogram may be different. All of these have been implemented with an efficient computer program in this proposed scheme. Figure 3 shown below is an illustration of histogram modification.

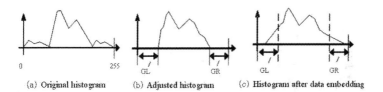

(a) Original histogram   (b) Adjusted histogram   (c) Histogram after data embedding

Fig. 3. Histogram modification

4   Proposed Reversible Data Hiding Algorithm

In this section, prior to presenting our proposed new method, we first discuss thresholding method developed in our previous work because it is relevant.

4.1   Thresholding Method

To avoid the possible underflow and/or overflow, often only the wavelet coefficients with small absolute value are used for data embedding [4]. This is the so-called thresholding method, which first sets the threshold T depending on the payload and embeds the data into those IWT coefficients with $|x| \leq T$. It does not embed data into the wavelet coefficients with $|x| > T$. Furthermore, for all high frequency wavelet coefficients with $|x| > T$ we simply add T or $-T$ to x depending x is positive or negative so as to make their magnitude larger than

Table 2. Formulas of thresholding method for reversible data hiding. x': gray levels after embedding, $\lfloor x \rfloor$: rounds x to the largest integer not larger than x.

parts of histogram	Embedding		Recovering	
	after embedding	condition	after recovering	condition
Data hiding region (right side) (positive or zero)	$x' = 2x + b$	$x \leq T$	$x = \lfloor \frac{x'}{2} \rfloor, b = x' - 2x$	$x' \leq 2T - 1$
Data embedded region (left side) (negative)	$x' = 2x - b$	$-T \leq x$	$\lfloor \frac{(x'+1)}{2} \rfloor, b = x' - 2x$	$-2T - 1 \leq x'$
No data embedded region (right edge part) (positive)	$x' = x + T + 1$	$x > T$	$x = x' - T - 1$	$x' > 2T + 1$
No data embedded region (left edge part) (negative)	$x' = x - T - 1$	$x < -T$	$x = x' + T + 1$	$x' < -2T - 1$

$2T$. In this way, the data embedding into coefficients with $|x| \leq T$ will not be confused with the large coefficients in which there is no data embedding. Therefore, the so-called thresholding method [4] is in fact the *minimum* thresholding method. The formulas of the thresholding method are shown in Table 2.

4.2   Optimum Thresholding Method Based on Histogram Pairs

As shown below, however, the minimum threshold T does not necessarily lead to the highest PSNR of mark image for a given payload. (This was also reported in [5].) The reason is as follows. If a smaller threshold T is selected, the number of coefficients with $|x| > T$ will be larger. These coefficients need to be moved away from the center of histogram by $(T+1)$ (refer to Table 2) in order to create histogram pairs to embed data. This may lead to a lower PSNR owing to moving a larger end part of the histogram. On the other hand, if a larger T is selected, more coefficients having larger magnitude are to be changed for data embedding, possibly resulting in a lower PSNR of the marked image. Instead of arbitrarily picking up some threshold T (as the starting point for data embedding) and some stopping point S for stopping data embedding as done in [5], it is found that for a given data embedding capacity there does exists an optimum value for T. In this proposed optimum histogram pair reversible data embedding, the best threshold T for a given data embedding capacity is searched with computer program automatically and selected to achieve the highest PSNR for marked image. This will be discussed in Section 5.

The proposed method divides the whole histogram into three parts: (1) the1st part where data is to be embedded; (2) central part - no data embedded and the absolute value of coefficients is smaller than that in the 1st part; (3) the end part - no data embedded and the absolute value of coefficients is larger than that in the 1st part. The whole embedding and extraction procedure can be expressed by the formulae in Table 3. There T is the selected threshold, i.e., start position for data embedding, S is stop position, x is feature (wavelet coefficient) values

Table 3. Formulas of optimum thresholding method of reversible data hiding

parts of histogram	Embedding		Recovering	
	after embedding	condition	after recovering	condition
Data hiding region (right side) (positive or zero)	$x' = 2x + b - \|S\|$	$\|S\| \leq x \leq T$	$x = \lfloor \frac{(x'+\|S\|)}{2} \rfloor, b = x' + \|S\| - 2x$	$\|S\| \leq x' \leq 2T - 1 - \|S\|$
Data embedded region (left side) (negative)	$x' = 2x - b + \|S\| + u(S)$	$-T \leq x \leq -\|S\| - u(S)$	$\lfloor \frac{(x'-\|S\|-u(S)+1)}{2} \rfloor, b = x' - \|S\| - u(S) - 2x$	$-2T - 1 + \|S\| + u(S) \leq x' \leq -\|S\| - u(S)$
No data embedded region (central part) (small absolute value)	$x' = x$	$-\|S\| - u(S) < x < \|S\|$	$x = x'$	$-\|S\| - u(S) < x' < \|S\|$
No data embedded region (right edge part) (positive)	$x' = x + T + 1 - \|S\|$	$x > T$	$x = x' - T - 1 + \|S\|$	$x' > 2T + 1 - \|S\|$
No data embedded region (left edge part) (negative)	$x' = x - T - 1 - \|S\| + u(S)$	$x < -T$	$x = x' + T + 1 - \|S\| - u(S)$	$x' < -2T - 1 + \|S\| + u(S)$

before embedding, $u(S)$ is unit step function (when $S \geq 0$; $u(S) = 1$; when $S < 0$; $u(S) = 0$); $\lfloor x \rfloor$ rounds x to the largest integer not larger than x. A simple example is presented in Section 4.5 to illustrate these formulas.

4.3 Data Embedding Algorithm

The high frequency subbands (HH, HL, LH) coefficients of IWT are used for data embedding in this proposed method. Assume the number of bits to be embedded is L. The data embedding steps are listed below.

(1) For a given data embedding capacity, apply our algorithm to the given image, to search for an optimum threshold T as shown in Figure 7 in Section 5. And set the $P \leftarrow T$. Where T is like a starting value.

(2) In the histogram of high frequency wavelet coefficients, move the portion of histogram with the coefficient values greater than P to the right-hand side by one unit to make the histogram at $P+1$ equal to zero (call $P+1$ as a zero-point). Then embed data in this point.

(3) If some of the to-be-embedded bits have not been embedded yet, let $P \leftarrow (-P)$, and move the histogram (less than P) to the left-hand side by 1 unit to leave a zero-point at the value $(-P - 1)$. And embed data in this point.

(4) If all the data have been embedded, then stop embedding and record the P value as the stop value, S. Otherwise, $P \leftarrow (-P - 1)$, go back to (2) to continue to embed the remaining to-be-embedded data, where S is a stop value. If the sum of histogram for $x \in [-T, T]$ is equal L, the S will be zero.

4.4 Data Extraction Algorithm

The data extraction is the reverse of data embedding. Without loss of generality, assume the stop position of data embedding is S, $S > 0$.. Steps are as follows.

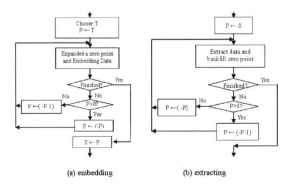

(a) embedding   (b) extracting

Fig. 4. Flowchart of proposed reversible data embedding and extracting

(1) Set $P \leftarrow S$.

(2) Decode with the stopping value P. Extract all the data until $P + 1$ becomes a zero-point. Move all the histogram greater than $P + 1$ towards the left-hand by one unit to cover the zero-point.

(3) If the extracted data is less than L, set $P \leftarrow (-P - 1)$. Continue to extract data until it becomes a zero-point in the position $(P - 1)$. Then move histogram (less than $P - 1$) towards the right-hand side by one unit to cover the zero-point.

(4) If all the hidden bits have been extracted, stop. Otherwise, set $P \leftarrow -P$, go back to (2) to continue to extract the data.

4.5   A Simple Yet Complete Example

In this simple yet complete example, the to-be-embedded bit sequence D=[1 10 001] has six bits and will be embedded into an image by using the proposed histogram pair scheme with threshold $T = 3$, and stop value $S = 2$. The image 5×5 shown in Figure 5 (a) has 12 distinct feature (grayscale) values, i.e., $x \in \{-5, -4, -3, -2, -1, 0, 1, 2, 3, 4, 5, 6\}$.

Figure 6 and Table 5 use solid (orange) line squares to mark the third histogram pair. The first histogram pair $[1, 0]$ is used to embed the 1st bit 1, the second histogram pair $[0, 2]$ is used to embed the next two bits 1,0 , and the third histogram pair $[3; 0]$ is used to embed three bits: 0,0,1.

During expanding, we are first making $h(4) = 0$, then making $h(-4) = 0$, finally making $h(3) = 0$. Note that $h(3) = 0$ at this time makes $h(4) = 0$

0	4	0	-4	1		0	6	0	-5	1		0	6	0	-5	1
0	2	-2	3	-1		0	2	-2	4	-1		0	2	-2	5	-1
4	-3	0	2	-3		6	-3	0	2	-3		6	-4	0	2	-3
-1	-2	0	-1	0		-1	-2	0	-1	0		-1	-2	0	-1	0
-2	1	2	-1	1		-2	1	2	-1	1		-2	1	3	-1	1
(a)						(b)						(c)				

Fig. 5. 5×5 wavelet subband (a) original one, (b) after 3 expanding, (c) after 6-bit embedding (what marked is how the last 3 bits are embedded)

Table 4. Formulas of reversible data hiding in the example in Section 4.5

	Embedding		Recovering	
	after embedding	condition	after recovering	condition
central	$x' = x, x' = [2, -1, 0, 1]$	$if - 2 < x < 2, x = [-2, -1, 0, 1]$	$x = x', x = [-2, -1, 0, 1]$	$if - 2 - u(S) < x' < \|S\|, x'=[-2,-1,0,1]$
right end	$x' = x + 2, x' = [6]$	$if x > 3, x = [4]$	$x = x' - 2, x = [4]$	$x' > 5, x' = [6]$
left end	$x' = x - 1, x' = [-5]$	$if x < -3, x = [-4]$	$x = x' + 1, x = [-4]$	$x' > -4, x' = [-5]$
right to be embedded	$x' = 2x + b - 2, b = 0 : x' = [2, 4], b = 1 : x' = [3, 5]$	$if 2 \le x \le -3, b = 0 : x = [2, 3], b = 1 : x = [2, 3]$	$x = \lfloor \frac{x'+2}{2} \rfloor, b = 0 : x' + 2 - 2x, b = 0 : x = [2, 3], b = 1 : x = [2, 3]$	$if 2 \le x' \le 5, b = 0 : x' = [2, 4], b = 1 : x = [3, 5]$
left to be embedded	$x' = 2x - b + 3, b = 0 : x' = [-3], b = 1 : x' = [-4]$	$if - 3 \le x \le -3, b = 0 : x = [-3], b = 1 : x = [-3]$	$x = \lfloor \frac{x'-2}{2} \rfloor, b = 0 : x' - 3 - 2x, b = 0 : x = [-3], b = 1 : x = [-3]$	$if - 4 \le x' \le -3, b = 0 : x' = [-3], b = 1 : x = [-4]$

Table 5. Formulas of histogram pair data embedding example $(T = 3, S = 2)$ (6 bit sequence D=[1 10 001]) (What marked is how the last 3 bits are embedded)

X		-5	-4	-3	-2	-1	0	1	2	3	4	5		6
h_0 (original)				1	2	3	4	6	3	3	1	2		
h_1 (extended)		1		0	2	3	4	6	3	3	1	2		
h_2 (embedded)		1		1	1	2	4	6	3	2	1	0	1	2
embedded (ordering)		no embedding		[1 0] embedded (second)		no embedding			[0 0 1] embedded (third)		[1] embedded (first)		no embedding

"shifting" to $h(5) = 0$. During each zero-point creation, the histogram shifting towards one of two (left and right) ends is carried out, the resultant histogram becomes $h_1 = [1, 0, 2, 3, 4, 6, 3, 3, 0, 1, 0, 2]$ (refer to Figure 5(b) and 2nd row of Figure 6). There histogram pairs are thus produced: in the right-most $h = [1, 0]$, in the left $h = [0, 2]$ and in the right (near center) $h = [3, 0]$.

After data embedding with bit sequence D=[1 10 001] and the selected scanning order, the histogram becomes $h_2 = [1, 1, 1, 2, 4, 6, 3, 2, 1, 0, 1, 2]$ (refer to Figure 5(c) and 3rd row of Figure 6). The three histogram pairs changed: in the right most from $h = [1, 0]$ to $h = [0, 1]$, in the left from $h = [0, 2]$ to $h = [1, 1]$, and in the right (near center) from $h = [3, 0]$ to $h = [2, 1]$.

After embedding, the grayscale values changed too. For example, embedding the last three bits (001) causes the right histogram pair (near center) to change from $h = [3, 0]$ to $h = [2, 1]$, and three grayscale values marked with small rectangles to change from $X = [2, 2, 2]$ to $X = [2, 2, 3]$ (refer to Figure 5 (c) and 3rd row of Figure 6).

Through this example, it becomes clear that the threshold can also be viewed as the starting point to implement histogram pair reversible data hiding. The formulas associated with this example are shown in Table 4, which provides a specific illustration of general formulas in Table 3.

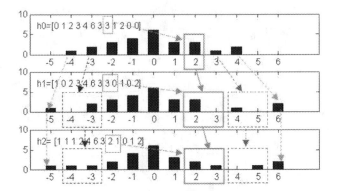

Fig. 6. Histogram pair data embedding example ($T = 3, S = 2$ to-be-embedded bit sequence D=[1 10 001]). What marked in solid (orange) line squares shows how the last 3 bits are embedded.

4.6   Data Embedding Capacity

Data embedding capacity L can be calculated as follows. When the stopping value S is negative: $L = \sum_{-T}^{S} h(X) + \sum_{-S}^{T} h(X)$; when S is positive or zero: $L = \sum_{-T}^{-S-1} h(X) + \sum_{S}^{T} h(X)$; and when S is zero: $L = \sum_{-T}^{-1} h(X) + \sum_{0}^{T} h(X) = \sum_{-T}^{T} h(X)$.

5   Selection of Optimum Parameters

For a given required data embedding capacity, the proposed method selects the optimum parameter to achieve the highest possible PSNR. The optimum parameters include: the best threshold T, the adaptive histogram modification value, G (in spatial domain), and the suitable data embedding region R. That is, optimal parameters can be selected as follows.

$$[T, G, R] = \arg_{T,G,R} \max{(PSNR)} \qquad (2)$$

(1) Best threshold T: Figure 7 shows the PSNR of marked image vs the threshold T with embedding capacity 0.02 bpp. It is observed there does exist an optimal threshold T for each of the three commonly used images: Lena, Baboon and Barbra.

(2) Adaptive modification value G: the histogram modification is carried out in this method adaptively "on real time", instead of as a necessary preprocessing in [4,5]. That is, after data embedding into each wavelet coefficient, underflow and/or overflow is checked. If underflow and/or overflow occurs, and it occurs from the left side (< 0), the left end of the histogram will be shrunk towards the center by an amount GL. GR is similarly handled. Our experiments have shown that on three frequently used test images: Lena, Barbra and Baboon, only when the embedding data rate is high than certain amount it needs histogram

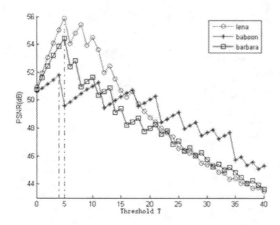

Fig. 7. Selection of the best threshold T

modification ($G > 0$). Otherwise, there is no need for histogram modification. This adaptive histogram modification leads to the higher PSNR of marked image for a given payload.

(3) Suitable data embedding region R: in order to improve the PSNR when the payload is small (e.g., < 0.1 bpp), we choose to only embed data into the HH subband , i.e., $R = \{HH\}$. When the payload is large, all three high frequency subbands are used, i.e., $R = \{HH, HL, LH\}$. This measure further enhances the PSNR for a given payload. Our experimental works have shown that the PSNR achieved by this new method is obviously better than that by the method [5] when the payload is rather small.

6   Experiments

In this section, we first present our experimental results by using the proposed method, which consists of two parts. The first part is experiments on three commonly used images, i.e., Lena, Barbra and Baboon images. The second part is one of the JPEG2000 test images, i.e., Woman image. Then, the results are compared with prior arts. Finally experimental results using Haar wavelet transform and using (5,3) integer wavelet transform are presented and compared.

6.1   Experimental Results and Performance Comparison

On three commonly used test images: Lena, Barbra and Baboon
For Lena, Barbra and Baboon three commonly used images (all in 512×512), we compare the results of our proposed histogram pair technique with that results of other techniques, i.e., techniques of [1,2,3,4,5,6,7,8,9]. The results of performance comparison are shown in Figures 8, 9 and 10, respectively. What shown in Figure 10(a) are the original Lena image and the marked Lena images generated by

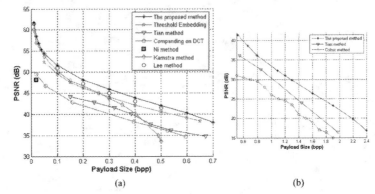

(a)   (b)

Fig. 8. (a) Performance comparison on Lena (b) Comparison of multiple-time data embedding into Lena image among [2], [8] and the proposed method

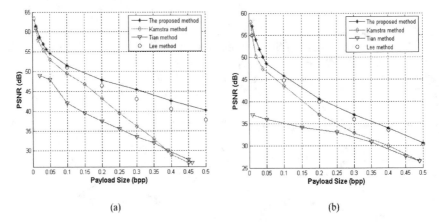

(a)   (b)

Fig. 9. (a) Comparison on Barbara (b) Comparison on Baboon

using the proposed method with the same group of three different payloads as used in [2], in Figure 10(b), the corresponding test results of [9] are shown. From these figures, it is observed that the PSNR achieved by our proposed method for the same embedded payload is the highest among the nine methods for these three commonly used test images.

Note that the platform used in all of experiments reported in Section 6 is as follows. CPU: Pentium 2.8GHz, RAM: 512M, OS: Windows XP SP2, and Matlab 7.0.

In Table 6, the three parameters, GR, GL, and G, are listed when applying our proposed adaptive histogram modification method to the above-mentioned three commonly used images with various embedding rates. It is interesting to observe the following. That is, our extensive experiments have shown that only when the embedding data rate for Lena is greater than 1.0 bpp, for Barbara greater than 0.57 bpp, and for Baboon greater than 0.008 bpp, it needs histogram modification

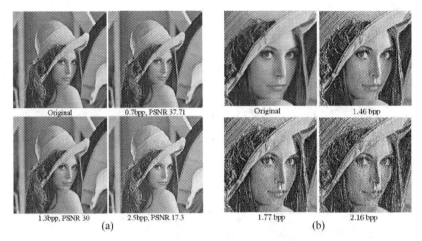

Fig. 10. (a) Original and marked Lena image with three different payloads by the proposed method (b) Performance on Lena image reported in [9]

Table 6. GL and GR values used in our experiments

Fig. 6 (a),6 (b),10 Lena					Fig. 7 (a) Barbara					Fig. 7 (b) Baboon				
bits	bpp	GL	GR	G	bits	bpp	GL	GR	G	bits	bpp	GL	GR	G
3132	0.0119	0	0	0	2819	0.0108	0	0	0	1037	0.0040	0	0	0
6744	0.0257	0	0	0	6041	0.0230	0	0	0	2089	0.0080	0	0	0
11986	0.0457	0	0	0	13064	0.0498	0	0	0	5082	0.0194	2	0	2
21206	0.0809	0	0	0	20095	0.0767	0	0	0	14936	0.0570	6	0	6
36421	0.1389	0	0	0	31729	0.1210	0	0	0	31148	0.1188	8	0	8
58672	0.2238	0	0	0	42639	0.1627	0	0	0	55990	0.2136	10	0	10
82720	0.3156	0	0	0	66702	0.2544	0	0	0	80122	0.3056	13	0	13
109009	0.4158	0	0	0	98430	0.3755	0	0	0	99015	0.3777	15	0	15
135062	0.5152	0	0	0	119672	0.4565	0	0	0	125005	0.4769	18	0	18
172983	0.6599	0	0	0	133784	0.5103	0	0	0	141066	0.5381	22	0	22
207273	0.7907	0	0	0	150320	0.5734	0	0	0					
285027	1.0873	0	0	0	174944	0.6674	0	3	3					
317999	1.2131	2	4	6	180910	0.6901	5	15	18					
336236	1.2826	6	22	28										
430482	1.6422	22	24	46										
510079	1.9458	42	48	90										

$(G > 0)$. Otherwise, there is no need for histogram modification when reversibly embedding data into these three commonly used images.

The PSNR versus payload, and parameters for multiple loop data embedding on Lena image are shown in Table 7.

Woman image

Woman image, one of the popularly used JPEG2000 test images, and its histogram have been shown in Figure 11. The histograms of three popularly used

Table 7. Multiple loop of data embedding into Lena image

Payload (bpp)	PSNR	Number of Loop	T for 1st Loop	T for 2nd Loop	T for 3rd Loop	T for 4th Loop	GL for 1st Loop	GR for 1st Loop	Block keeping for 1st Loop	Time (second)
1.3	29.7709	3	-6	-12	-3	No	6	6	33	2.8600
1.6	26.3727	3	-7	-22	-4	-4	35	42	1356	6.6100
1.9	23.2216	4	-8	-28	-14	-4	70	80	7512	11.0930
2.2	19.8060	4	-8	-28	-28	-9	127	147	27558	17.7180
2.4	16.8659	5	-9	-26	-40	-26	84	87	1264	42.4530

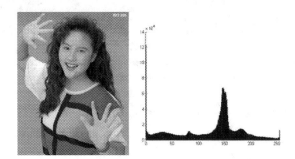

Fig. 11. (a) Woman image (b) its histogram

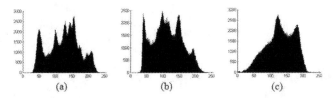

Fig. 12. Histogram of (a) Lena, (b) Barbra and (c) Baboon images

images in reversible data hiding research, i.e., Lena, Barbra and Baboon images are shown in Figure 12 (a), (b) and (c), respectively. It is observed that the both right and left ends of the histogram of Woman image have been occupied and with some high peaks, while the histograms of the three commonly used test images in the reversible data hiding community have both ends empty. Furthermore, Lena image has two ends empty most widely, while Barbra and Baboon images have two ends relatively narrower. These characteristics of three histograms explain why the histogram shrinking from both right and left ends are not necessary when the embedding rate is low for these three images. That is, GR and GL values are both equal to 0 as embedding rates are low. Hence, it is felt that it is necessary to test reversible data hiding algorithms on Woman image as well in order to have complete and objective performance evaluation of various reversible data hiding schemes.

Table 8. Performance of location map method [2] on Woman image

Payload (bpp)	PSNR (db)	T	Location map (bit)	Time (sec.)
0.09	43.6	10	809040	6.1
0.15	41.1	15	737024	6.3
0.19	39.1	20	679128	6.1
0.22	37.6	25	628520	7.0
0.24	36.4	30	582576	6.3
0.31	33.3	50	448088	6.1
0.36	30.8	∞	341328	6.0

Table 9. Performance of proposed method on Woman image

Payload (bpp)	PSNR (db)	T	S	Bookkeeping (bit)	GL	GR	Time (sec.)
0.01	57.5	3	-3	19176	1	1	12.8
0.10	49.1	2	0	62882	3	3	20.5
0.15	48.1	1	0	71616	3	5	20.4
0.20	45.9	1	0	98486	5	5	23.1
0.25	44.4	2	0	130909	6	8	26.6
0.30	42.9	2	0	170844	7	9	51.2
0.35	41.0	3	0	242053	10	11	69.7
0.40	39.4	4	0	301941	12	13	78.1

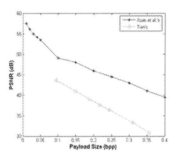

Fig. 13. Payload vs PSNR on Woman image

6.2   Comparison by Using Integer (5,3) and Haar Wavelets

Table 10 and Table 11 list the PSNR of marked image versus payload (bpp), and parameters of G, T, and S of the proposed reversible data embedding when using integer (5,3) and Haar wavelet, respectively. As expected, integer (5,3) wavelet provides higher PSNR for a given payload than integer Haar wavelet, while integer Haar is simpler in implementation. Specifically, as payload is as low as 0.05 bpp, for these three commonly used test images, the PSNR of marked versus original images achieved by using integer (5,3) is, respectively, 1.7 dB, 2.5 dB and 0.5 dB higher than that by using Haar IWT; as payload is 0.5 bpp, the

Table 10. PSNR of reversible data embedding using (5,3) IWT

Payload (bpp)	Lena				Barbara				Baboon			
	T	S	PSNR	G	T	S	PSNR	G	T	S	PSNR	G
0.05	3	-2	54.4	0	2	1	54.6	0	3	0	48.6	3
0.1	2	1	51.6	0	2	1	51.5	0	3	0	45.9	3
0.2	1	0	48.2	0	2	-1	47.8	0	4	0	40.6	6
0.3	2	0	46.0	0	2	0	45.3	0	6	0	37.0	10
0.4	3	0	43.9	0	4	0	42.6	0	9	0	34.0	18
0.5	4	0	42.1	0	5	0	40.2	0	16	0	30.6	30

Table 11. PSNR of reversible data embedding using Haar IWT

Payload (bpp)	Lena				Barbara				Baboon			
	T	S	PSNR	G	T	S	PSNR	G	T	S	PSNR	G
0.05	2	2	52.7	0	2	-2	52.1	0	7	-6	48.1	1
0.1	2	-2	50.1	0	2	1	46.9	0	5	3	43.6	3
0.2	3	-2	46.9	0	2	0	46.1	0	4	0	38.4	8
0.3	2	0	43.7	0	3	0	42.1	0	8	-1	35.0	15
0.4	4	-1	41.8	0	4	-1	40.2	0	11	0	31.9	21
0.5	6	-1	39.5	0	7	-1	37.1	0	17	0	29.1	28

PSNR by integer (5,3) is, respectively, 2.6 dB, 3.1 dB, and 1,5 dB higher higher than that by using Haar IWT.

7   Discussion and Conclusion

(1) In this paper, it has been shown that the minimum threshold T in reversible data hiding does not necessarily provides the best performance in terms of the visual quality of marked image measured by PSNR versus data embedding capacity.

(2) An optimum histogram pair based image reversible data embedding scheme using integer wavelet transform is presented in this paper. It uses the new concept of histogram pair to reversibly embed data into image. Furthermore, it is characterized by the selection of best threshold, adaptive histogram modification parameters and suitable embedding region. The experimental results have demonstrated its superior performance in terms of the visual quality of marked image measured by PSNR versus data embedding capacity, to our best knowledge, over all of the prior arts including [1,2,3,4,5,6,7,8,9].

(3) Different from the method in [5], our proposed method uses histogram pair to reversibly embed data, which provides more flexibility in implementation. The procedure of histogram pair is also used in adaptive histogram modification in an inverse way. That is, the same histogram pair technique is used in data embedding as well as in histogram modification to avoid overflow and underflow.

(4) Furthermore, the new method systematically and computationally selects the best threshold, the adaptive histogram modification parameters GR and GL, and the most suitable data embedding region.

(5) One example in selecting suitable data embedding region is for reversible data embedding into Lena image as the payload is low. Our experimental works have shown that the PSNR of marked image achieved by this new method is distinctly better than that achieved by the method [5] because the new method first selects integer wavelet coefficients in the HH subband for data embedding as the payload is low instead of embedding data arbitrarily into the wavelet coefficients of the HL, LH and HH subbands.

Furthermore if the payload is further low such that not all of the high-frequency coefficients in the HH subband need to be used for data embedding, an additional measure is adopted to further raise the PSNR of marked image versus original image. That is, the magnitudes of all of the wavelet coefficients in the immediate next-level HH_1 wavelet subband are examined so as to arrange these coefficients in an non-increasing order according to their magnitudes. In addition to the proposed optimum histogram pair scheme described above, the data is sequentially embedded into those wavelet coefficients in the original-level HH subband, which correspond to the magnitude non-increasing order arranged in the immediate next-level HH_1 subband. This measure has been shown effective in further raising the PSNR of marked Lena and Barbara images as the payload is rather low.

(6) The computational complexity, including optimal histogram pair based data embedding and possible histogram modification, is shown affordable for possible real applications. Specifically, for data embedding ranging from 0.01 bpp to 1.0 bpp into three commonly used images: Lena, Barbara and Baboon, the execution time varies from 0.25 to 2.68 seconds with the platform of CPU: Pentium 2.8GHz, RAM: 512M, OS: Windows XP SP2, and Matlab: 7.0.

(7) If the data embedding rate is not high (e.g., as shown in Table 6, not higher than 1.0873 bpp for Lena image, 0.5734 bpp for Barbara image, and 0.0080 bpp for Baboon image), the amount of histogram modification G = 0, meaning that the histogram shrinking is not needed. This means that when the data embedding rate is not larger than a specific amount for a given image, our proposed reversible data hiding method does not need to calculate point-by-point to avoid the possible underflow and/or overflow as required in the methods proposed in [2] or [3]. Under this circumstance, the proposed reversible data hiding becomes very simple in implementation.

(8) To the authors' best knowledge, for the first time in the literature, one of the JPEG2000 test images, Woman, has been used in experimental study for reversible data hiding. This is necessary since the histogram of Woman image is quite different from these three frequently used test images: Lena, Barbra and Baboon images. The histogram of Woman has peaks at both grayscale values 0 and 255, while the histograms of the three frequently used images do not have these two end values occupied. It is shown that our proposed method can still effectively and efficiently work for Woman image.

(9) In our experimental works, the proposed method has been applied to both integer (5,3) and Haar wavelet transforms. It is shown that using integer (5,3) wavelet brings out better performance in terms of data embedding rate versus PSNR. The proposed method can also be applied to any other integer wavelet transforms, demonstrating its flexibility is using integer wavelet transforms. Note that the reversible method in [2] can only use Haar transform.

Acknowledgement

Authors sincerely thank Ms. Haifeng Xiao and Mr. Patchara Sutthiwan for their time and efforts put into the preparation of this paper at the very early and very final stages, respectively.

References

1. Ni, Z., Shi, Y.Q., Ansari, N., Su, W.: Reversible data hiding. IEEE Transactions on Circuits and Systems for Video Technology 16(3), 354–362 (2006)
2. Tian, J.: Reversible data embedding using a difference expansion. I EEE Transactions on Circuits and Systems for Video Technology, pp. 890–896 (August 2003)
3. Kamstra, L., Heijmans, H.J.A.M.: Reversible data embedding into images using wavelet techniques and sorting. IEEE transactions on image processing 14(12), 2082–2090 (2005)
4. Xuan, G., Shi, Y.Q., Yang, C., Zheng, Y., Zou, D., Chai, P.: Lossless data hiding using integer wavelet transform and threshold embedding technique. In: IEEE International Conference on Multimedia and Expo (ICME 2005), Amsterdam, Netherlands, July 6-8 (2005)
5. Xuan, G., Shi, Y.Q., Yao, Q., Ni, Z., Yang, C., Gao, J., Chai, P.: Lossless data hiding using histogram shifting method based on integer wavelets. In: Shi, Y.Q., Jeon, B. (eds.) IWDW 2006. LNCS, vol. 4283, pp. 323–332. Springer, Heidelberg (2006)
6. Yang, B., Schmucker, M., Funk, W., Busch, C., Sun, S.: Integer DCT-based reversible watermarking for images using companding technique. In: Proceedings of SPIE, Security and Watermarking of Multimedia Content, Electronic Imaging, San Jose, CA, USA (January 2004)
7. Lee, S., Yoo, C.D., Kalker, T.: Reversible Image Watermarking Based on Integer-to-Integer Wavelet Transform. IEEE Transactions on Information Forensics and Security 2(3), part 1 (September 2007)
8. Coltuc, D., Chassery, J.M.: Very fast watermarking by reversible contrast mapping. IEEE Signal Processing Letters 14(4), 255–258 (2007)
9. Coltuc, D.: Improved capacity reversible watermarking. In: International Conference on Image Processing (ICIP), San Antonio, Texas,USA, September 16-19, 2007, pp. III-249–III-252 (2007)

Author Index